Don Schmierer

WITH LELA GILBERT

Celebrating
God's
Design

A BALANCED & BIBLICAL
PERSPECTIVE ON TODAY'S
TOUGHEST YOUTH ISSUES

Contents

Introduction

You have in your hands a great resource for helping students deal with gender identity issues in a sensitive, biblically based manner. *Celebrating God's Design* has been written to help you draw students into discussions about difficult, yet important topics that are of deep concern for them as they are daily bombarded with the confusing and immoral messages of the culture. It will give students the tools to see themselves and others from the perspective of their loving Father God's eyes and to deal in a biblical way with the moral dilemmas facing them.

Each session is made up of several components:

Warm Up is a short clip from the accompanying videotape. These clips are designed to immediately draw students into the session topic.

Real Life is a true story that will allow students to emotionally engage the topic and explore their own feelings.

Team Effort is designed to get students talking in smaller groups of three to five to exchange ideas and learn from one another.

In the Word leads students into a discussion of Father God's perspective of the topic by exploring His Word.

Things to Think About is designed to further the discussion and help students apply what they have learned.

Father God Reflection Time is an opportunity to bring the focus back to the author and finisher of our faith—Father God—by wrapping up the session in corporate prayer. It also is an opportunity for the leader to encourage students to take home the Father God handout to reflect on at home during the week.

God bless you as you endeavor to lead your students to learn God's perfect design for human sexuality.

Celebrating God's Unique Design

Then God said, "Let us make people in our image, to be like ourselves. They will be masters over all life—the fish in the sea, the birds in the air, and all the livestock, wild animals, and small animals." So God created people in his own image; God patterned them after himself, male and female he created them.

-Genesis 1:26,27

Thank you for making me so wonderfully complex! Your workmanship is marvelous—and how well I know it. You watched me as I was being formed in utter seclusion, as I was woven together in the dark of the womb. You saw me before I was born. Every day of my life was recorded in your book. Every moment was laid out before a single day had passed. How precious are your thoughts about me, O God! They are innumerable!

-Psalm 139:14-17

Notable Quotes

"The important question is not whether God 'exists'; it is whether God cares about us, and whether we need to care about God's purposes." [Phillip E. Johnson, *Defeating Darwinism* (Downers Grove, InterVarsity Press, 1997) p. 17.]

Note: This curriculum is based on the truth that God created and designed all things including humankind and is personally involved in every human life. For further information on this issue, please refer to Phillip Johnson's excellent book (cited above).

Key Ideas

God created us, male and female, according to His special design and loving intention. He did so to bring honor and delight to Himself. He allows each of us to have strengths and weaknesses so He can include us in the work he is doing. God is not only our Designer and Creator; He is our Father, and His love for us is the love of a perfect father for a beloved child.

WARM UP

10 Minutes

- View the video.
- Distribute "God's Unique Idea" handout.
- Have students complete the page and discuss.

REMINDER: Inform students that handouts are not to be turned in. Discuss them, then they may keep or dispose of them.

REAL LIFE

10 Minutes

BETTY'S STORY

• Share the following real-life story.

Even though God created the human race perfectly, and even though He has a perfect plan for our lives, nobody is perfect. We all have physical, emotional, intellectual or spiritual things about ourselves that we wish were different. And yet we know that God created us uniquely, with a specific purpose, just the way we are.

Here's a real-life story:

Betty was an only child. She was born into a very strict religious family, and her parents were in their late 30s when she was born. They were old fashioned, critical and their love was usually conditional—Betty had to be good to earn it.

To make matters worse, Betty had a chronic skin disease that caused her to itch constantly. Her scratching was uncontrollable, and her skin was always scabby and peeling off in flakes. Every part of her was slightly swollen from this condition, and consequently she was not very attractive. In fact, even though her condition was not contagious or infectious, people often got up and moved away from her, and they were afraid to touch things she had touched. Although she went to many doctors, no one seemed able to help her.

Betty's personality was warped by her constant rejection, both at home and in social settings. Her parents repeatedly told her that she was lazy, irresponsible and rebellious. Betty's peers made fun of her appearance and her emotional overreactions, and it was true that she was emotionally unstable. She cried easily, raged occasionally and developed a very cynical, negative attitude. She had few friends and her home life was as lonely as her life at school because she never really felt welcome there. She had crushes on boys and daydreamed about them, but no one ever looked her way. Although

she was a Christian believer, it was very hard for Betty to imagine a loving God. First of all, her parents were not loving people. Secondly, why would a loving God allow her to suffer so much?

When she was 16 years old, Betty heard a message that really got her attention. It said that God made each person according to His perfect plan, and that every person should thank Him for being the unique person he or she is. The teaching also said that God had placed each person in the home of His choosing for His reasons.

- Distribute "Betty's Story" handout.
- Have students complete the page and discuss in small groups or with the whole group. After the discussion, conclude with the following:

Betty's story is a true story, although her name has been changed to protect her identity. Here's what happened to Betty.

After hearing that message, Betty went to the front of the church and prayed with a pastor, asking God to change her life and her attitude. She began to thank God for being different and learned to appreciate her uniqueness, difficult as it was. Five years later, the Lord healed her skin, and she discovered a new life.

TEAM EFFORT

10 Minutes

- Distribute "God's Perfect Creation" handout.
- Instruct students to complete the handout.
- Have students form groups of three to five.
- Give groups one minute to write down as many things they can think of that a person can change about him- or herself (i.e., hair color, clothing, where they live, etc.).
- Give groups one minute per category to write down as many examples as they can think of.
- Have groups share a few examples in each category as you discuss the following:

The things we'd like to change about ourselves usually fall into three categories:

1. **Things we *can* change (if we work hard, seek help or use self-discipline)**

(This category might include things such as weight, physical looks, short tempers, bad grades, sexual sins, or not-so-great reputations.) **God can help us find answers for these things by sending the right people, information or solutions into our lives. He has promised to provide wisdom if we ask for it** (see James 1:5).

2. **Things we *cannot* change**

These might include birth defects, chronic illnesses, ethnicity, level of intelligence, lack of athletic coordination, etc. **God can mold our character and teach us to rely on Him for strength and success if we give our unchangeable weaknesses to Him** (see 2 Corinthians 12:9).

3. **Things we *don't need* to change because, even though someone else has criticized or labeled us or we have found fault with ourselves, they really aren't true or even important.**

Discussion here can be very helpful to those who have been labeled by parents or peers, or by those who have a distorted view of themselves. You might want to point out things such as thinking we're fat or stupid or clumsy or gay or other untruths we believe because of insults. Also, some things will change on their own as we grow up, such as height, family problems, etc.

- Use the following object lesson to demonstrate our worth to God.

Pull out a brand new dollar bill (or a 5-, 10- or a 20-dollar bill) and ask: **How much is this worth?** Now wad the bill up, stomp on it, mark it with a pen—whatever you can think to do to the bill, yet retain its value—then ask: **What is the bill worth now?** Continue: **If a dollar bill is rumpled or stomped on or damaged in some other way, it will not be quite the same afterward. It may be** wrinkled or torn or faded. But it still retains its original value. This dollar is worth what it is worth because a higher authority has given it its value. The same is true of us. No matter what we've been through, God has given us inestimable value, and no one can take that value from us. God has told us to turn to other Christians for guidance and direction and in doing so we gain wisdom and truth (see Proverbs 11:14).

IN THE WORD

15 Minutes

• Read the following and discuss the questions:
Genesis 2:19: *So the LORD God formed from the soil every kind of animal and bird. He brought them to Adam to see what he would call them, and Adam chose a name for each one.*

Father God brought Adam into a trusting partnership, and gave him dignity and responsibility by asking him to name all of the animals. If that first human had been you, and your Father had given you such an important and prestigious role...

Genesis 2:18: *And the LORD God said, "It is not good for the man to be alone. I will make a companion who will help him."*
Genesis 2:23: *"At last!" Adam exclaimed. "She is part of my own flesh and bone! She will be called 'woman' because she was taken out of a man."*

How would you have felt about yourself?

How would you have felt toward Father God?
Father God identified Adam's real felt need for a companion and did what He had to do to meet that need.

What type of feelings do you think Adam had toward his new wife/companion?

What type of feelings do you think Adam had toward Father God?

Genesis 2:24. *This explains why a man leaves his father and mother and is joined to his wife, and the two are united into one.*

What gender of people did God bring together to establish a family?

Matthew 19:4-6: *"Haven't you read the Scriptures?" Jesus replied. "They record that from the beginning 'God made them male and female.'" And he said, "This explains why a man leaves his father and mother and is joined to his wife, and the two are united into one. Since they are no longer two but one, let no one separate them, for God has joined them together."*

Why do you think Jesus affirmed God's two-gender creation?

THINGS TO THINK ABOUT

5 Minutes

Questions teenagers sometimes ask:

Q. Sometimes I get really angry at God for making me the way I am. There are some bad things about myself that I can't change, and I don't understand. Why didn't He give me a better break?

A. The first thing that you need to remember is that God loves you more than anyone will ever love you, and that God never makes mistakes. He created you the way you are for His purposes, for His delight, and so that He can use your strengths and weaknesses to help you become more like Jesus.

One of the things we learn from our challenges, handicaps and limitations is to rely on God for strength and capability. Another thing we learn is compassion. We also learn to view life in a deeper, more meaningful way rather than simply as a pursuit of pleasure. And we discover our own uniqueness in the things that make us different than others.

God made you the way you are because He loves you. And He is able to do more for you than you can possibly imagine if you will completely rely on Him. (see Ephesians 3:20)

Q. My father (or mother) is very critical of me and doesn't even seem to love me. What can I do?

A. Parents aren't perfect, and they sometimes treat their children the way they were treated as children. The first thing we have to do in dealing with our parents is forgive them for their unkindness, their mistakes and their poor communication.

Most parents love their children, but that love gets hidden behind layers of criticism, disapproval and inability to communicate in a positive way. Some parents see another person in a child—an ex-spouse, a brother or sister, or even things they don't like in themselves. This may cause them to treat you unreasonably. Other parents were never shown affection, approval or attention when they were children, and they don't know how to demonstrate those things to you. Still others have problems with uncontrolled anger, physical exhaustion, alcohol and other extenuating circumstances.

Even after we forgive our parents, we remain wounded by the words they've said and the unkind things they've done. That's why it is so important for us to seek God's healing for our hurt, and to see God as a perfect parent, a heavenly Father who loves each of us unconditionally, wants only the best for us and never treats us unjustly or unreasonably. During the next few weeks as we continue this study, we can learn how to re-parent ourselves with God as our perfect parent.

Q. How do I know if I was born gay?

A. You aren't. There is no reliable evidence that anyone is born gay. And the Bible tells us that God doesn't want people to take part in homosexual behavior because of things that have happened to them. Obviously, He wouldn't say that something is wrong, and then create people who could only function that way.

You may be asking this question because you are attracted to homosexual behavior. And you may believe you are gay because you have been emotionally attached to someone of the same sex, or even because you have participated in a sexual act with a person of the same sex. Perhaps you were sexually molested as a child, and because of the complicated feelings involved, you assume you are homosexual. You may think you're homosexual because people have told you that you are, or because other kids taunt you by calling you "gay," "faggot" or "dyke."

None of these circumstances indicate that you are a homosexual. Why? Because homosexual behavior is a choice people make. You may, however, have some unanswered questions regarding your true, God-given gender. If so, you should talk to a trustworthy adult.

Father God Reflection Time

5 Minutes

Why do you suppose God allowed Adam to name the animals?

God did two things for Adam that demonstrated His love for His created son: First, He allowed Adam to name the animals. Second, He created a mate for Adam before Adam even realized he needed or wanted one. How do you think these things caused Adam to feel about his Father God?

God has told us to call Him "Abba" which is another way of saying "Daddy." Why do you think He wants us to call Him that?

• Distribute the Father God handout and explain that these are for students to take home and reflect on what they have learned today.

CLOSING PRAYER

Divide into small groups of three or four. Have group members pray for one another, thanking God for one good and special quality each person has.

God's Unique Idea

In your wildest imagination, can you envision a world where Father God made every person exactly alike? Every man would look identical to every other man; every woman would be a clone of every other woman. There would be no difference in eye color, hair color, size, personality or anything else!

1. Write some reasons why it was good for God to create each person unique and one-of-a-kind.

2. In what ways are human beings' problems, differences and challenges valuable to them?

3. Why do you think God's Word specifically says that He made humans male and female?

Who is able to advise the Spirit of the LORD? Who knows enough to be his teacher or counselor? **Isaiah 40:13**

Session 1

Betty's Story

1. Betty's parents were strict, cold and conditional in their love for her. Some parents are abusive and cruel. How do you think people like Betty feel about Father God?

2. Many of the problems Betty faced in her life were unchangeable. What things could she have changed? What could she not change?

3. Betty heard a message that reminded her that she was God's unique creation and that He chooses a specific family for each person. What are some of the ways Betty might have reacted to this message?

The LORD is like a father to his children, tender and compassionate to those who fear him. Psalm 103:13

Session 1

God's Perfect Creation

The things we'd like to change about ourselves usually fall into three categories:

1. Things we can change if we work hard, seek help or use discipline: How many can you think of?

2. Things we cannot change: How many can you think of?

3. Things we don't need to change because, even though someone else has criticized or labeled us or we have found fault with ourselves, they really aren't true or even important. How many can you think of?

> *Thank you for making me so wonderfully complex! Your workmanship is marvelous and how well I know it.* **Psalm 139:14**

Session 1

FATHER GOD

For you did not receive a spirit that makes you a slave again to fear, but you received the Spirit of sonship. And by him we cry, "Abba, Father." Romans 8:15 (NIV)

Did you know that God wants you to feel safe with Him and has invited you to call Him "Daddy"? That's what Abba means, and that's one of the ways He wants You to think of Him. Instead of being frustrated, scared or lonely, He wants you to run to Him in your fear, cry out to Him and rely on Him. He has promised to help you and comfort you.

How could thinking of God as your Daddy change the way you face the challenges in your life?

Write a prayer to Father God, thanking Him for being your heavenly Daddy.

Session 1

Debunking Some Myths

Now the serpent was the shrewdest of all the creatures the LORD God had made. "Really?" he asked the woman. "Did God really say you must not eat any of the fruit in the garden?"

"Of course we may eat it," the woman told him. "It's only the fruit from the tree at the center of the garden that we are not allowed to eat. God says we must not eat it or even touch it, or we will die."

"You won't die!" the serpent hissed. "God knows that your eyes will be opened when you eat it. You will become just like God, knowing everything, both good and evil." Genesis 3:1-5.

And Jesus said,
"And you will know the truth, and the truth will set you free." John 8:32

Notable Quotes

"To date, no researcher has claimed that genes can determine sexual orientation. At best, researchers believe that there may be a genetic component. No human behavior, let alone sexual behavior, has been connected to genetic markers to date." ["Why Ask Why? Addressing the Research on Homosexuality and Biology." Pamphlet distributed by P-FLAG, Parents and Friends of Lesbians and Gays; prepared with the assistance of professionals including Dr. Clinton Anderson of the American Psychological Association.]

Key Ideas

God created us, male and female, according to his special design and loving intention. God did not create homosexuals, although some people have been led to believe that they were born that way. Because Satan has introduced several myths in our culture about this subject, we need to be sure that we have our facts right. God has set boundaries around all kinds of human activities, including sexual behavior, and He allows us to make choices about those boundaries. However, no matter what boundaries we cross or what choices we make, it's important to understand that God always wants to reconcile with us.

WARM UP

10 Minutes

- Show video clip.
- Distribute "The First Big Myth" handout.
- Have students complete the page and discuss.

> **REMINDER:** Inform students that handouts are not to be turned in. Discuss them, then they may keep or dispose of them.

REAL LIFE

AMY'S AND JERRY'S STORIES

• Read the following stories:

When Amy was four years old, a neighbor boy sexually molested her. She didn't talk to her parents about it, because she thought it was her fault. Her father, who could be very critical and nonaffirming, had a difficult time dealing with girls. So he treated Amy more like a boy than a girl. Then, when she started school, Amy got in trouble for rubbing a kindergarten classmate's neck when he said he had a headache. Amy grew up feeling more and more ashamed of herself and especially ashamed of being a girl. Gradually, she began to act and dress like a tomboy. She stopped playing girl games and took on the role of a boy when playing with her friends. As she got older, she began to feel sexually attracted to girls, and by the time she was twenty-one, she was involved in a lesbian relationship.

Jerry's parents divorced when he was seven years old, and he was shattered when his father moved away and didn't keep in touch with him or his sister. After the divorce Jerry's mother leaned on him emotionally, confided in him, and took him everywhere with her. Jerry had learning disabilities, was physically delicate and not good at sports. He was called "sissy" and "fag" on the playground. In junior high Jerry attached himself emotionally to a male counselor that he was taken to. He wanted to ask the counselor to "come home with me and be my daddy." From that time on, he was emotionally attracted to males. At age 18, Jerry went to his first gay bar and became sexually active. From that time on he was involved in homosexual behavior.

- Distribute "Amy's and Jerry's Stories" handout.
- Have students discuss the questions.
- After the discussion, conclude with the following: Amy's and Jerry's stories are true, although their names have been changed to protect their identities. Here's what happened to Amy and Jerry.

Amy became a Christian when she was 20, and Jerry when he was 21. They both accepted Christ even though they were still actively involved in homosexuality. Before long, they each decided to seek help in finding their true sexual identities. Individually, they enrolled in a Christian one-year program that helps people who don't want to continue in homosexuality. Amy and Jerry met during the recovery program. After participating in intense spiritual and psychological therapy, they fell in love with each other. Two years later they were married. They've been together for ten years now, and they have two children.

TEAM EFFORT

15 Minutes

- Distribute "What Causes Homosexual Behavior" handout.
- Have students complete the page on their own or in small groups of three to five.
- Discuss the handouts in small groups and then share the following (for background information, please refer to *An Ounce of Prevention*, chapters 3 and 8):

COMMON MYTHS ABOUT HOMOSEXUAL BEHAVIOR

***Myth 1: Homosexual behavior is genetic—or like a third gender.* Myth 1 is the most common one in our culture. It is not true, and it causes a great deal of confusion. You need to know the real story about Myth 1.**

- Review NARTH sheet (see Appendix B) regarding genetics; highlight and discuss the key points of the sheet with students.

Myth 2: According to the Bible, homosexuality is okay. **Myth 2 is believed by some Christians and some churches. Although God's Word makes it very clear that all sins are displeasing to God and that we should not judge one sin more harshly than another, it also clearly states that homosexuality is wrong.**

- Ask students to look up the following verses and have volunteers read them aloud.

  Leviticus 20:13 (*NIV*): *"'If a man lies with a man as one lies with a woman, both of them have done what is detestable.'"*

  Leviticus 18:22 (*NIV*): *"'Do not lie with a man as one lies with a woman: that is detestable.'"*

  1 Corinthians 6:9,10 (*NIV*): *Neither the sexually immoral nor idolaters nor adulterers nor male prostitutes nor homosexual offenders . . . will inherit the kingdom of God.*

  Romans 1:26,27 (*NIV*): *God gave them over to shameful lusts . . . their women exchanged natural relations for unnatural ones. In the same way the men also abandoned natural relations with women and were inflamed with lust for one another. Men committed indecent acts with other men, and received in themselves the due penalty for their perversion.*

Myth 3: Ten percent of the population is gay. **Myth 3 is incorrect. Based on recent studies, only about two to three percent of the population is actively involved in homosexual behavior.**

Myth 4: Homosexual behavior is an alternative lifestyle—a good, healthy choice for some people. **Myth 4 is untrue and dangerous. The homosexual lifestyle is not a safe alternative. It involves physical, emotional and spiritual dangers—some of them life-or-death risks.**

Myth 5: Once you decide to become involved in homosexual behavior, there is no way back—you can't change your direction. **Myth 5 is proved false by the lives of thousands of former gays and**

29

lesbians who have affirmed their true gender and left homosexual behavior behind.

Myth 6: Homosexuals are victims. Myth 6 is partly true. Many who get involved in homosexual behavior are victims of molestation and sexual abuse; most are victims of tragic family circumstances. But they are not victims of homosexuality itself. Homosexual feelings may not be a choice, but homosexual behavior is a chosen behavior. Homosexuality is not an unavoidable, unchangeable destiny.

IN THE WORD

15 Minutes

FIRST, THE BAD NEWS

- Use the following information to summarize Genesis 3:6-24:

  - Eve persuaded Adam to cross Father God's boundary and to disobey His instructions.
  - Adam and Eve felt ashamed and tried to hide from Father God.
  - Both of them blamed someone or something else for their actions.
  - They broke their relationship with Father God— no more walks and conversations in the garden with Him.
  - There were long-term consequences of their choices: Adam and Eve had to leave the beautiful garden; life would always be a struggle for them.

NOW THE GOOD NEWS

Father God introduced His plan for salvation from sin. In Genesis 3:15 He shared His plan for reconciliation with mankind.

"From now on, you and the woman will be enemies, and your offspring and her offspring will be enemies. He will crush your head, and you will strike his heel."

In this statement, God hints at a coming Redeemer. By using the word "he," God indicates that one person is meant. And since that time, only one descendent of Eve has been born of woman without being born of man—Jesus Christ. Jesus, who fulfilled Genesis 3:15, crushed the head of Satan when He died on the cross for the sins of all humankind, and then was resurrected by Father God's powerful love.

Father God had this plan even before He created the world for humankind:

> *For you know that God paid a ransom to save you from the empty life you inherited from your ancestors. And the ransom he paid was not mere gold or silver. He paid for you with the precious lifeblood of Christ, the sinless, spotless Lamb of God. God chose him for this purpose long before the world began, but now in these final days, he was sent to the earth for all to see. And he did this for you.* 1 Peter 1:18-20

> *The Lamb of God who was killed before the world was made.* Revelation 13:8

Do you think Father God really had joy in his relationship with Adam and Eve? Why or why not?

Father God treated Adam and Eve to the best anyone could ever have, affirming them, providing for every need, giving them the freedom to make choices and allowing them to give back loyalty to Him. What happened to this beautiful relationship that caused Adam and Eve to hide from God?

What choices have you made that you would like to have erased forever?

How does the thought of someone paying a high ransom in order to win back a broken relationship with you make you feel? Why would someone do that for you?

Things To Think About

Optional

"Do for others what you would like them to do for you." Matthew 7:12

• Discuss the following questions with the whole group.

Q. There's a gay guy at my school and I don't want to be seen with him because people will think I'm gay too. What am I supposed to do?

A. First of all, just because everybody calls someone gay doesn't mean it's true. And even if an adolescent identifies himself or herself as gay or a lesbian, he or she probably hasn't participated in a same-sex relationship. This is a trap vulnerable young people fall into, and by not being friendly to them, you may unintentionally increase the likelihood that they will eventually get involved in homosexual behavior.

There are always social outcasts around us, and Christians are specifically called to be loving and caring people. Many times it is social unacceptability that drives young people into homosexual relationships because they feel so lost and alone. Once you understand that people aren't born gay, you shouldn't feel so threatened by the bad choices they make, or by some hidden fear that you might have been born gay yourself. You weren't. Neither were they.

Q. Isn't saying homosexuality is wrong being homophobic?

A. There is an important principle to remember in dealing with people: Everyone needs loving support— someone to help them discover what is good and what is harmful. People who are abnormally fearful of homosexuals do not love the people involved. They mock them, shun them and sometimes even act violently against them. This is sometimes called "homophobia"and it is just as sinful as homosexuality.

Christian love is supposed to be demonstrated to all people at all times. It doesn't mean we condone their behavior. It doesn't mean we participate in their actions or pretend they are right. What it does mean is that we are kind to them; we try to show them that God loves them and that He wants them to live normal, healthy lives.

Q. If I'm nice to somebody who thinks he's gay (or she's a lesbian), will he (or she) put a move on me? What do I do if he (or she) does?

A. Look at it this way—don't you treat your opposite sex friends differently if you think you would like to go out with them than if you wouldn't? Most people recognize the difference between friendship and flirting. Just being nice to someone probably won't cause him or her to think you are interested in hooking up.

However, if you do find that someone has formed a same-sex emotional attachment to you, don't panic! It doesn't mean that you are gay or bisexual. It simply means that you should let him or her know that you aren't comfortable with the attachment, and that you want to be friends, but nothing more. Sometimes that even happens with people of the opposite sex—we have to let them know we aren't interested in a relationship, even if they are. It may hurt them a little at the time, but it prevents bigger hurts later on.

If a same-sex encounter like this occurs, it is, of course, important for you to let a trustworthy adult know about the situation. That way, help can be provided for the other person as soon as possible.

Father God Reflection Time

5 Minutes

• Distribute Father God handout for reflection at home.

CLOSING PRAYER

Guide students in prayer, asking Father God to help them discern between His truth and Satan's lies. Conclude with thanksgiving for God's gift of salvation through Jesus Christ's death on the cross.

The First Big Myth

THE SNAKE'S SET-UP

"Really?" he asked the woman. "Did God really say you must not eat any of the fruit in the garden?" (Genesis 3:1).

Consider the question the snake asked Eve and check off the reason you think he asked it.

- ☐ The snake was lonely and just wanted to have a conversation with the woman.
- ☐ The snake didn't mean to cause a problem—he just asked an innocent question.
- ☐ The snake had some doubts about God, and his question contained a half-truth.
- ☐ The snake had an evil hidden agenda—he had in mind a "bait-and-switch" scheme.
- ☐ None of the above: I think _____

EVE'S EXPLANATION

"Of course we may eat it" the woman told him. "It's only the fruit from the tree at the center of the garden that we are not allowed to eat. God says we must not eat it or even touch it, or we will die" (Genesis 3:2,3)

Consider Eve's response to the snake's question. She answered from her...

- ☐ Emotions.
- ☐ Intellect.
- ☐ Physical desire.
- ☐ Spiritual understanding.
- ☐ All of the above.
- ☐ None of the above: Eve was

THE SNAKE'S SEDUCTION

"You won't die!" the serpent hissed. "God knows that your eyes will be opened when you eat it. You will become just like God, knowing everything, both good and evil." The woman was convinced. The fruit looked so fresh and delicious, and it would make her so wise! (Genesis 3:4.5).

Think about Satan's myth. Why do you think Eve went ahead and ate the fruit?

> *"How could I ever do such a wicked thing? It would be a great sin against God."* **Genesis 39:9**

Session 2

Amy & Jerry's Stories

1. Amy didn't tell anyone about her molestation because she blamed herself. What are some other reasons sexual abuse victims don't report the things that happen to them?

2. In your opinion, what are some of the things in Jerry's background that set the stage for his choice to get attracted to and involved in homosexual behavior?

3. What are some reasons a guy or a girl might become confused about his or her gender?

Lead me by your truth and teach me, for you are the God who saves me. All day long I put my hope in you. **Psalm 25:5**

Session 2

What Causes Homosexual Behavior

Circle T for true or F for false.

BIOLOGICAL FACTORS

T F Homosexuality is genetic—determined by DNA. It's like a third gender.

T F There are homosexual tendencies—sort of like alcoholic tendencies.

T F There are no biological causes. It's a sin—period.

T F It might be hormonal with some people.

PARENTS AND FAMILY

T F Homosexuality has nothing to do with family background.

T F Homosexuality is caused by a weak, mousy mom/overbearing father.

T F Homosexuality is caused by an absent dad/domineering mom.

T F Homosexuality is rebellion because of an overprotective, too-close family.

T F Dad wanted a girl and got a boy, or vice versa.

T F Homosexuals are often best friends with their same-sex parent.

T F Homosexuals are caused by parents who abused drugs in the 60s.

ABUSE AND CRISES

T F Homosexuality often begins with sexual abuse or molestation.

T F Homosexuality is the result of satanic rituals.

T F Homosexuality is caused by the shock of having a death in the family.

T F Homosexuality is only a moral choice, and it has nothing to do with abuse or crises.

SOCIAL FACTORS

T F Most homosexuals were well adjusted as children.

T F Low self-esteem can be a factor in homosexual choices.

T F Peer pressure can lead to homosexual behavior.

T F Homosexuality is the result of drinking or doing drugs.

> *Because you are sons, God sent the Spirit of his Son into our hearts, the Spirit who calls out, "Abba, Father." Galatians 4:6 (NIV)*

FATHER GOD

"God is not a man, that he should lie. He is not a human, that he should change his mind. Has he ever spoken and failed to act? Has he ever promised and not carried it through?" Numbers 23:19

Think about the following statements, and ask yourself if you really believe them deep in your heart:
- **Father God will never lie or deceive me.**
- **Whatever God says, I can completely trust it to be true.**
- **God will not tell me one thing, then change His mind later.**
- **I can always count on Father God as a loyal friend.**
- **Father God desires a personal, intimate relationship with me.**

What difference would it make in your life if you knew you could trust Father God with every aspect of your life, no matter what?

Write a prayer to Father God, thanking Him that He is always trustworthy, always available and that He wants a personal relationship with you. Ask Him to help you remember these statements about His faithfulness to you.

Session 2

Media & Me

Don't copy the behavior and customs of this world, but let God transform you into a new person by changing the way you think. Then you will know what God wants you to do, and you will know how good and pleasing and perfect his will really is. Romans 12:2

"Media's influence on our children plays an undisputed role. By the time the average child graduates from high school, they will have watched up to 26,000 hours of television, 5,000 of those hours by the first grade. They will have seen between 240,000 to 480,000 sexual acts or references to sex, between 800,000 to 1.5 million acts of violence, and between 192,000 to 360,000 murders." [*Citizen's Courier*, Summer 1998, p. 4.]

Key Ideas

God has called us to be in the world but not of the world. He wants us to help free people who are caught in the world's traps, but He also wants us to avoid those traps ourselves. His plan is to remake us from the inside out into the image of Christ. That involves His continuous working in us and our cooperating with Him by refusing to conform to the world's ways.

WARM UP

20 Minutes

- Show the video.
- Ask students to share their reactions to the video. Allow several to comment.
- Discuss the video with the whole group.

> **REMINDER:** Inform students that handouts are not to be turned in. Discuss them, then they may keep or dispose of them.

REAL LIFE

10 Minutes

ERIC'S STORY

- Share the following real-life story.

At the age of 21, Eric gave into a desire he'd had for a long time. He went to an adult bookstore and watched some pornographic movies with homosexual content. On the way out, a man came on to him, and because he was still aroused by the movies, Eric allowed the man to do what he wanted. This was his first sexual experience with a man.

Eric was a Christian, and afterwards he was heartbroken by what he had done. He confessed his sin, asking God to forgive him. "I promise never to do it again," he told the Lord.

But Eric didn't tell anyone else, didn't ask anyone to pray with him, and was too ashamed and afraid of rejection to get support from other Christians.

It wasn't long before he was back at the bookstore and involved in another encounter. This quickly became an addictive pattern of behavior for Eric. He continued to live a double life for 10 years, keeping straight friendships with other Christians, while secretly having anonymous gay sex with strangers. Eric was deeply torn and ashamed of himself. He became extremely depressed and attempted suicide more than once.

One night Eric was in a terrible car accident and he ended up in a hospital with serious injuries. During his hospitalization, a Christian pastor went to see him. Eric confessed what he had been doing to the pastor and prayed for forgiveness. But a blood test taken when he was admitted, revealed that Eric was infected with the HIV virus.

- Distribute "Eric's Story" handout.
- Have students complete the page and discuss as a whole group.
- After the discussion, conclude with the following:

Eric's story is a true story, although his name has been changed to protect his identity. Here's what happened to Eric.

After Eric rededicated his life to God in the hospital, he made a decision to get help in dealing with the things in his life that led to his belief that he was gay. A Christian therapist counseled him for three years, and by the time his therapy was finished, he had overcome his desire for porn and for homosexual behavior. After that, he started a Christian recovery organization for people struggling, as he had, with addictions to pornography and gay sex. Today he speaks everywhere about his new life with AIDS . . . and Jesus.

TEAM EFFORT

15 Minutes
- Distribute "The Ways of the World" handout.
- Have students form groups of three to five.
- Have students complete the page on their own; then discuss the two questions in their small groups.

Take a minute or two to challenge students about what changes they would consider making in their personal involvement with various forms of media. Are they willing to commit to making those changes? Ask them to write on the back of the handout one change they are willing to make this week.

IN THE WORD

15 Minutes
- Share the following with the whole group.

The importance of not conforming to the world's ways is made clear throughout the Bible. One Bible character named Daniel was tested about conformity in an extreme way. We can find Daniel's story in Daniel 1—4.

Daniel was taken as a captive from his country Israel—a country that had received abundant blessings, prosperity and protection from Father God. However, the people of Israel, as a whole, disrespected Father God by ignoring or disobeying what He asked them to do. They insulted and hurt Him by acting in ways that went against His good character and nature. After many years of warning from God's spokesmen, His prophets, God withheld His hand of blessing and protection from Israel, allowing many of the people, along with Daniel, to be taken captive to a foreign kingdom called Babylon.

The people of Babylon grieved the heart of Father God by worshiping idols and living in wickedness. Their lives were extravagant and luxurious beyond imagination, but with all their wealth, they totally disregarded the common people's need. The poverty of Babylon's poor was terrible.

When we serve Father God, we often have to

make tough choices, but they bring about good results. During Daniel's time in Babylon, he had to do just that.

- Distribute "Stranger in a Strange Land" handout.
- Complete and discuss the handout in small groups or with the whole group.
- Continue to explain:

Here are some examples of Daniel's tough choices:

- Read (or ask a volunteer read) Daniel 1:19,20.

The Results: Daniel's godly choice caused the king of Babylon to appoint him as an advisor, after which the king found Daniel's wisdom 10 times greater than that of his peers.

- Read (or ask a volunteer read) Daniel 2:12-19.

It was a tough choice for Daniel to stand up for Father God's honor. And he was not afraid to place his life on the line even when all his peers failed and their lives were doomed.

- Read (or ask a volunteer read) Daniel 2:47.

The Results: Daniel's uncompromising faith caused Daniel's God to be honored: "'Truly, your God is the God of gods, the Lord over kings, a revealer of mysteries, for you have been able to reveal this secret.'"

- Read (or ask a volunteer to read) Daniel 3:13-18.

Another tough choice was faced when Daniel and his friends were bold and did not conform by bowing down to worship a golden image of the king. They didn't obey even after they were threatened to be thrown in the fiery furnace. They defied the king's command and were willing to die rather than serve or worship any god except their own God.

- Read (or ask a volunteer read) Daniel 3:28-30.

The Results: God rescued His servants who trusted in Him. This caused the king of Babylon to give praise to the God of Daniel and his friends. They were promoted to even higher positions in Babylon by the king.

- Read (or ask a volunteer read) Daniel 4:19,27.

Yet another tough choice: In order to stand up for truth and righteousness, Daniel had to give really bad news to the king. He had to confront him and tell him to stop sinning. He challenged the king to break with his past and to be merciful to the poor.

- Read (or ask a volunteer read) Daniel 4:34.

The Results: The king of Babylon praised and worshiped Father God as the King of heaven and earth.

Father God Reflection Time

5 Minutes

Why do you think God allowed Daniel's three friends to be thrown in the fiery furnace even though they were being obedient to Father God?

Why do you think God allowed Daniel to be thrown into the lion's den?

Sometimes Father God allows us to be in difficult situations so He can better demonstrate to us His love and care. Often, it is when we are at the end of our own resources, plans and strategies that we turn our eyes toward Him. Only then are we able to see how much He loves us.

- Distribute Father God handout for reflection at home.

CLOSING PRAYER

- Form small groups of three to five. Have students pray for one another, asking God to help them find the courage to stand up for God's ways in an often challenging world. Have them pray for any commitments they might have made regarding the temptations they are trying to resist.

Eric's Story

1. Eric gave in to a temptation he'd struggled against for a long time. What could have helped him win the battle against that temptation?

2. Eric could have had emotional support and help from his Christian friends if he'd told them about his struggle with pornography and homosexuality. Why do you think he was afraid to tell them?

3. How do you think you would react if one of your friends told you he or she was struggling with homosexuality?

"Father, I have sinned against both heaven and you, and I am no longer worthy of being called your son." Luke 15:21

Session 3

The Ways of the World

Although you may not be influenced by the same things as your friends or classmates, some kind of temptation may be trying to catch you in one of many traps. Which of the following is most likely to influence your thinking? Mark as many as apply to you—no one will see your paper.

- ☐ Movies
- ☐ Music
- ☐ MTV/Music videos
- ☐ Television dramas/comedies
- ☐ Video games
- ☐ Commercials
- ☐ School programs
- ☐ Pornography
- ☐ Internet
- ☐ Teachers
- ☐ Newspapers and magazines
- ☐ Opinions of celebrities

- ☐ Other _____
- ☐ Other _____
- ☐ Other _____

Discuss the following with your small group.

1. Describe a time when you were influenced to do something—good or bad—by some form of media.

2. What do you think is the best way for Christians to keep these influences from affecting them personally?

> *Let heaven fill your thoughts. Do not think only about things down here on earth.* **Colossians 3:2**

Session 3

Stranger in a Strange Land

> Because Daniel had been taken by force to Babylon, he had to face some difficult emotional challenges.

1. Can you recall a time when you felt like an outsider, like you didn't belong or like a captive? What were your feelings/reactions to this situation?

> Having to change his name further demoralized Daniel. His original name "Daniel" reflected his Father God because it meant "God is judge." The new name given to him by his Babylonian captors—"Belteshazzar"—was repulsive to his faith because it meant "may Bel protect his life" referring to a Babylonian god. He was also forced to learn to speak the language of his captors.

2. Being put down or demoralized is a very painful thing. Can you recall a time or two when that happened to you? How did you feel and what did you do?

> After all this, the pressure increased on Daniel to compromise his faith in Father God and to conform to the Babylonian culture.

3. It takes a great deal of determination to stand up for what you believe in. Can you recall a time when you were able to do that? What happened?

> *I can do everything with the help of Christ who gives me the strength I need.* **Philippians 4:13**

Session 3

FATHER GOD

*But suddenly, as he was watching, Nebuchadnezzar
jumped up in amazement and exclaimed to his advisers,
"Didn't we tie up three men and throw them into the fire?"
"Yes," they said, "we did indeed, Your Majesty."
"Look!" Nebuchadnezzar shouted. "I see four men
unbound, walking around in the fire. They aren't even hurt
by the flames. And the fourth looks like a divine being."*
Daniel 3:24,25.

**Did you know that Father God goes with you into every
circumstance you face? Not only does God protect you and
defend you, He stands with you, walks with you and even faces
your greatest challenges with you. You probably won't actually
see Him, the way the three friends and the king did, but He has
promised never to leave you or forsake you.**

How could knowing that Father God is always with you make a
difference in your life?

Write a prayer to Father God, thanking Him for His protection. Ask
Him to help you live in a way that demonstrates the reality of His
love and protection.

Session 3

Making Love Last

Don't you know that your body is the temple of the Holy Spirit, who lives in you and was given to you by God? You do not belong to yourself, for God bought you with a high price. So you must honor God with your body. 1 Corinthians 6:19,20

God wants you to be holy, so you should keep clear of all sexual sin. 1 Thessalonians 4:3

"Teenagers do, however, have at least two deep personal reasons for getting involved in premarital sex. Whether I talk in a junior high, at a high school assembly, or at a university, I preface almost every talk by pointing out: 'Almost every single one of you has two fears. One is the fear that you'll never be loved, and the other is the fear you will never be able to love." [Josh McDowell and Dick Day, *How to Be a Hero to Your Kids* (Dallas: Word Publishing, 1991) p. 117.]

Key Ideas

God created human beings—male and female. From the beginning He planned for women and men to be together as couples, even telling Adam, "It is not good for you to be alone." Sexual relationships were designed by God, and He has instructed his people to carry them out in the context of the marriage of one man to one woman. Christians should submit to God's instructions about sexuality because His ways are best and because our bodies are the temple of His Spirit.

WARM UP

10 Minutes

- Show the video.

> **REMINDER:** Inform students that handouts are not to be turned in. Discuss them, then they may keep or dispose of them.

REAL LIFE

10 Minutes

SHELLEY'S STORY

- Share the following real-life story.

Shelley and her parents were thrilled beyond belief when she received her acceptance letter from Princeton University—one of the most difficult schools in the country to get into. It had been Shelley's dream to go to Princeton since elementary school, so her father immediately wrote the check for the deposit and mailed it that same day. Then he and Shelley's mom took Shelley and her boyfriend Jeff out to dinner at a beautiful restaurant, where they joyfully celebrated her big accomplishment.

Shelley and Jeff were Christians, and although they had dated for two years, they had never had sexual intercourse. The night of the senior prom, they went out with several couples and enjoyed reminiscing about their years of school together. Someone had brought a bottle of champagne, and everyone toasted the future. Shelley normally didn't drink but, "After all," she thought, "this is my senior prom, and I may never see some of these kids again." Jeff drank occasionally, and he was quite happy to have a couple of glasses of champagne.

After the dance, all the seniors headed for a local hotel, where several rooms had been rented so they could party all night. More alcohol appeared from various backpacks and handbags, and before long everyone was at least a little drunk. Couples were kissing and going off together alone, and—to make a long story short—Shelley and Jeff ended up having sex for the first time.

A few weeks later, Shelley was horrified to realize that her period was late. In a panic, she rushed out and bought a home pregnancy test and took it into a bathroom at a gas station. It was positive!

Jeff and his family had gone on vacation, so she couldn't talk to him. Shelley didn't know where to turn for help. Her first impulse was to have an abortion and not tell anyone. But she didn't have any money, and she wasn't sure she could live with that idea anyway.

After several days of agonized indecision, Shelley finally told her parents. They were heartsick but supportive. They prayed with Shelley and convinced her that she shouldn't have an abortion—she should have the baby, and either give it up for adoption or keep it herself.

Shelley had to give up her lifelong dream. She wrote a regretful letter to Princeton University, informing them that she would not be able to attend there after all. She and Jeff talked about marriage, but neither of them thought they were ready for it. He went away to school that fall; Shelley stayed home, got a part-time job.

- Distribute "Shelley's Story" handout.
- Have students complete the page and discuss.
- After the discussion, conclude with the following.

Shelley's story is a true story, although her name has been changed to protect her identity. Here's what happened to Shelley

After Shelley's baby girl was born, Shelley started taking a few classes at a local junior college. But working part time, trying to study and take care of a baby proved too difficult for her. She gave up on her education, and decided to focus her attention on her little daughter. Although, as years went by, she was promoted at work and eventually made a fairly good income, Shelley never returned to school, never pursued her dream, and—so far—has never married.

TEAM EFFORT

10 Minutes

- Distribute "God's Plan for Sex" handout.
- Have students form small groups of three to five, then complete and discuss the page.
- Discuss the following with the whole group:

What are the repercussions of sexual misbehavior?

What is adultery? How does it differ from premarital sex?

Is sexual behavior private or does it involve the whole community? Why or why not?

Do you think morality has changed in the past few years? Why or why not?

IN THE WORD

15 Minutes

NOT DOING WHAT COMES NATURALLY

- Share the following summary:

Here's a glance into the Hebrew patriarch Joseph's life from Genesis 39:7-23 and 41:37-40.

1. Joseph was a very handsome, well-built young man who was taken captive and sold into slavery by his brothers.

2. Joseph was bought by Potiphar. Potiphar's flirtatious wife often hit on him, trying to get him to have sex with her.

3. Joseph responded by saying, "Your husband trusts me and it would be a sin against my Father God."

4. On one occasion, when he refused to sleep with her, he rushed for the door. She grabbed his tunic and ripped it off as he ran from her.

5. Feeling rejected and angry, Potiphar's wife falsely accused Joseph of rape, using his tunic as evidence, and got him thrown in jail.

6. For a time it appeared that Joseph had been foolish to have honored Potiphar and God.

Even in jail, Joseph trusted in God, and asked God for wisdom when he was asked to interpret the dreams of some of his fellow inmates. After he interpreted the dreams for Pharaoh, this is what happened:

Then Pharaoh said to Joseph "Since God has made all this known to you, there is no one so discerning and wise as you. You shall be in charge of my palace, and all my people are to submit to your orders. Only with respect to the throne will I be greater than you." So Pharaoh said to Joseph, "I hereby put you in charge of the whole land of Egypt. Then Pharaoh took his signet ring from his finger and put it on Joseph's finger. He dressed him in robes of fine linen and put a gold chain around his neck. He had him ride in a chariot as his second-in-command, and men shouted before him, "Make way!" Thus he put him in charge of the whole land of Egypt. (Genesis 41:39-43, NIV)

The following are some of the positive consequences of Joseph's "not doing what comes naturally."

1. Father God honored Joseph and promoted him to the number one position of power and authority under Pharaoh.

2. Because God had given him wisdom, Joseph was able to save his new country from the disaster of a severe famine.

3. Joseph's brothers, who sold him into slavery came to him for food, were forgiven and asked to live with him. And Joseph was reunited with his grieving father, Jacob, and received his blessing.

THINGS TO THINK ABOUT

Optional

- Distribute "Doing What Comes Naturally" handout.
- Discuss with the whole group.
- Option: Have students discuss handout in the same small groups formed in Team Effort.

FATHER GOD
REFLECTION TIME

5 Minutes

Do you think being used by Father God is a good thing?

Why is being used by God different from being used by selfish people?

- Distribute Father God handouts for reflection at home.

CLOSING PRAYER

Have students form small groups of three or four. Invite them to pray for one another, asking God for help and discernment about areas of sexual temptation and weakness.

Shelley's Story

1. Shelley's parents loved her very much; her boyfriend was a Christian, and he cared for her too. She was intelligent, pretty and popular. Who or what should be blamed most for Shelley's heartbreaking situation?

2. What would you have done differently if you were in a situation similar to Shelley's?

What would you have done the same?

3. What do you think Jesus would say to Shelley if she were face-to-face with Him?

Don't let the excitement of youth cause you to forget your Creator. Honor him in your youth before you grow old and no longer enjoy living. Ecclesiastes 12:1

Session 4

God's Plan For Sex

1. God clearly designed men and women to be together in every way. They fit together emotionally, spiritually and physically. But He wanted them to be married to one another before they experienced sexual oneness. Write some reasons why you think God designed sex to be appropriate only within a marriage between a man and a woman.

2. Check the things that you think make it difficult in our society for young men and women to wait for sex until marriage.

- ☐ Movies
- ☐ Videos
- ☐ Song lyrics
- ☐ Anything-goes morality
- ☐ Sexually-focused advertisements
- ☐ Hormones
- ☐ Dating
- ☐ Fashion styles
- ☐ Contraceptives
- ☐ Sex education
- ☐ Social pressure
- ☐ Alcohol and drugs
- ☐ People who have sex and don't get into trouble
- ☐ Other

Do you think your staying a virgin is as important to you as it is to your parents? Explain.

> *Show me the path where I should walk, O LORD; point out the right road for me to follow.* **Psalm 25:4**

Session 4

69

Doing What Comes Naturally

1. We are often torn between doing what is right according to Father God's instructions, and doing what we feel like doing. In fact, our natural response may be just the opposite of what God expects of His adopted children. Considering the ways in which Joseph was victimized, what could have been a natural response? What do you think he felt like doing about ...

His brothers, who sold him into slavery?

The new country and new family he served while in slavery?

Father God, who didn't seem to care about him?

2. If Joseph had done what comes naturally, what might have been some consequences of his actions with . . .

Potiphar's flirtatious wife?

Potiphar?

His new undesirable home, the jail?

How can I know all the sins lurking in my heart? Cleanse me from these hidden faults. Keep me from deliberate sin. Psalm 19:12,13

Session 4

FATHER GOD

In a wealthy home some utensils are made of gold and silver, and some are made of wood and clay. The expensive utensils are used for special occasions, and the cheap ones are for everyday use. If you keep yourself pure, you will be a utensil God can use for his purpose. Your life will be clean, and you will be ready for the Master to use you for every good work. Run from anything that stimulates youthful lust. Follow anything that makes you want to do right. Pursue faith and love and peace, and enjoy the companionship of those who call on the Lord with pure hearts.
2 Timothy 2:20-22

Father God is proud of you and He wants to put you to work in His kingdom. His desire is for you to be like an exquisite utensil made from gold and silver, used to serve His very important guests. He wants you to be a fine instrument in His hands, able to accomplish His purposes and display His loving nature for all the world to see. He really loves you, but the decision to be a utensil of finest quality gold and silver—or something of lesser quality—is yours to make.

Knowing that Father God wants your very best, is there an unnecessary temptation in your life right now from which you ought to be running away? What might that be?

Write a prayer to Father God thanking Him for making you a special instrument to serve Him. Ask Him to help you run from temptation.

Session 4

Prescriptions for Peace with Parents - I

"Honor your father and your mother, as the LORD your God has commanded you. Then you will live a long, full life in the land the LORD your God will give you." Deuteronomy 5:16

"Honor your father and mother." This is the first of the Ten Commandments that ends with a promise. And this is the promise: If you honor your father and mother, *"you will live a long life, full of blessing."* Ephesians 6:2,3

"The strength of a nation . . . is the strength of its families. It is not a strong nation that makes families safe. It is the strong families that make a nation prosperous. The family is both a refuge and a launching point for change in society." [Pastor Mike McIntosh, quoted by Jane Hansen, *Fashioned for Intimacy* (Ventura, CA: Regal Books, 1997) p.26.]

Key Ideas

God purposely designed men and women to bear children, and thus to keep the human race growing and expanding on the earth. Besides physical childbearing, men and women are also given the responsibility of feeding, clothing, sheltering, teaching and—most of all—loving their children. And God has instructed children to honor their parents. Although this can be challenging because of the sinful and selfish nature of humans, it is the task of Christian young people to obey God's instruction and to work toward an understanding and loving relationship with their parents—even the most difficult ones.

WARM UP

10 Minutes

- Show the video.

> **REMINDER:** Inform students that handouts are not to be turned in. Discuss them, then they may keep or dispose of them.

REAL LIFE

10 Minutes

BRIAN'S STORY

- Share the following real-life story.

Brian was an unusual boy—he was very gifted in mathematics and physics, and was a creative thinker. However, by the time he reached 14 years of age he clearly lacked some of the most basic social and personal skills. He was hard to talk to, and his parents were deeply disappointed in what they called Brian's "weirdness."

There was a continual state of tension in Brian's home, with many arguments, slammed doors and days of the silent treatment. Brian's mother repeatedly told her son that she

simply didn't like him, and that she wished he were a completely different person. His father traveled constantly and rarely spoke to Brian when he was home.

It was fairly obvious to all who knew him that Brian was dealing with an ever-increasing state of depression. Although Brian wasn't a Christian, he had several Christian friends who tried to encourage him and lift his spirits. Finally, in desperation, his mother asked him to move out. He went to live alone in an apartment that was managed by his grandfather. He was 16 years old, and although his parents bought his groceries and paid his bills, they sometimes did not contact him for weeks at a time.

It seemed to his friends and teachers that Brian's despair was increasing, but no matter who talked to him or his parents, there was no end to their bitter resentment toward each other. As Brian's depression deepened and he began to talk about suicide, school officials became increasingly alarmed. They confronted the parents, urging them to reconcile with their son. A psychiatric counselor prescribed antidepressant medication. And at last his mother reluctantly told Brian he'd have to move back home.

- Distribute "Brian's Story" handout.
- Have students complete the page and then discuss with the whole group.
- After the discussion, conclude with the following:

Brian's story is a true story, although his name has been changed to protect his identity. Here's what happened to Brian:

Brian moved home on Friday night. John, one of his Christian friends who had given him clothing, spent hours keeping him company and prayed for him continually, spent the weekend with Brian. John was sad to see that the mother barely spoke to Brian and the father was out of town. John pleaded with Brian not to think about suicide and to look forward to the future—Brian had been selected to be class

valedictorian and had been offered physics
scholarships at several first-tier universities.
John went home Sunday night to get ready for
school on Monday. Brian didn't show up at
school that day. Monday night Brian had
hanged himself—in a location where his
mother would be the first person to find him.

TEAM EFFORT

15 Minutes

- Distribute "Dealing with Parents" handout.
- Have students form three or more small groups.
- Assign each small group one of the three scenarios
  to discuss. If you have more than three groups, it's
  all right to assign the scenarios more than once.
- Allow a few minutes for each small group to share
  their responses with the whole group.

Note: It is important to encourage participants to
know that their conversations in this setting will be
kept in strictest confidence—both by adult leaders
and students. It would also be wise for you to find
adult support (but not parents of the students) for
the discussions this week and next week. You
might consider making arrangements in advance
with qualified church members—preferably
couples—who will step into any difficult situations
that surface during these sessions. **This would
be a good opportunity to discuss the
Confidentiality Agreement (see appendix A)
and have students complete and sign it.**

IN THE WORD

15 Minutes

- Share the following information on Joseph's life.

    We have looked at a time in Joseph's life when
he was tempted by sexual sin. Now we are going to
consider his godly behavior toward his family.
Here's a quick sketch of Joseph's life from Genesis
37—50.

- **Joseph's relationship with his father, who was controlling and over-protective**

- **The jealousy between Joseph and his brothers**

- **The wrath of Joseph's brothers, resulting in selling him into slavery**

- **How Joseph dealt with anger and rejection— with faith in God, loyalty and hard work**

- **Joseph's promotion to honor and a position of leadership**

- **How God used Joseph to save a foreign nation**

- **Joseph's refusal to take revenge, even when given the opportunity**

- **The God-honoring relationship Joseph built with his father and brothers**

Joseph has set a wonderful example for all of us to follow in dealing with family troubles. He was forgiving, gracious and generous—even after all the bad things that were done to him. But that was then and this is now: What about today?

- Distribute "Learning from Joseph" handout.

- Instruct students to discuss the handout in their small groups.

- Assuring them that their comments will be kept in confidence, invite them to share their answers with the whole group.

*FATHER GOD
REFLECTION TIME*

5 Minutes

**Is it difficult for you to imagine Father God as a
loving, caring parent whose arms are always open
to you?**

**Do you realize that He is always listening, is never
annoyed with your mistakes and is forever willing to
forgive your every sin and mistake?**

CLOSING PRAYER

Invite students to stand in a circle, hold hands and pray
for one another and for all the families represented in
the group.

Brian's Story

1. Have you ever felt completely unloved? Explain.

2. What, if anything, could Brian have done differently to deal with his parents' lack of love and understanding?

3. What should kids do when they are facing really unkind, unloving or otherwise unbearable situations at home?

What should friends, teachers and others do about someone who has a difficult home situation?

Share each other's troubles and problems, and in this way obey the law of Christ. **Galatians 6:2**

Session 5

Dealing with Difficult Parents

God's ideal is that parents and children should: love one another; forgive one another; take care of one another; support one another; and pray for one another. But in a sinful world, that's not always the way things work out. Just as parents sometimes have to figure out how to deal with difficult kids, kids may have to find a way to live peaceably with difficult parents.

Scenario One: Your parents are control freaks. They want to know everything you do, everywhere you go and even everything you think. Describe some godly ways that you can build trust with your too-controlling parents.

Scenario Two: Your parents are one continuous episode of Family Feud. They continually argue, fight and bicker. As a Christian teenager, describe some ways that you can cope with parents who don't get along.

Scenario Three: Your parents are missing in action. They are either home but disinterested, never home at all, drunk, detached or depressed. How can you find a godly solution to this lonely situation?

Don't let anyone think less of you because you are young. Be an example to all believers in what you teach, in the way you live, in your love, your faith, and your purity. 1 Timothy 4:12

Session 5

Learning from Joseph

Page 1

Can you remember a time when you ever felt mistreated or misunderstood by your family? (**Note:** Your answers will be kept completely confidential):

1. I have felt misunderstood and really hurt by _____ when . . .

2. I felt anger and hatred toward _____ because . . .

3. I still have _____ feelings toward _____ because . . .

4. I'm dealing with my anger by . . .

5. Forgiveness is hard/easy for me because . . .

6. Joseph faced many challenges in his family and he came through them in a godly way. What can you learn from him?

Session 5

Learning from Joseph

Page 2

7. If I had been in Joseph's shoes and sold into slavery by my brothers or sisters, I would have . . .

8. If I had been thrown in jail because I was framed by a lustful, vindictive person, I would have . . .

9. If the same brothers or sisters who sold me into slavery showed up years later, wanting food from me, I would . . .

10. I think Joseph was . . .

> *"As far as I am concerned, God turned into good what you meant for evil. He brought me to the high position I have today so I could save the lives of many people. No, don't be afraid. Indeed, I myself will take care of you and your families." And he spoke very kindly to them, reassuring them.* **Genesis 50:20,21**

Session 5

FATHER GOD

LORD, you know the hopes of the helpless. Surely you will listen to their cries and comfort them. You will bring justice to the orphans and the oppressed, so people can no longer terrify them." Psalm 10:17,18 (NIV)

Try to imagine a time when you have a chance to visit with Father God. He is very happy to see you when you walk into the room—His face breaks into a smile at the sight of you. He invites you to sit down with Him, and He explains that He would like for you to describe the hurts you are feeling. He puts His arm around you to comfort you, and He is listening to your every word.

What would you say to Him?

Dear Father God,

Love,
Your Adopted Child

Prescriptions for Peace with Parents - II

"Honor your father and your mother, as the LORD your God has commanded you. Then you will live a long, full life in the land the LORD your God will give you." Deuteronomy 5:16

"Honor your father and mother." This is the first of the Ten Commandments that ends with a promise. And this is the promise: If you honor your father and mother, "you will live a long life, full of blessing." Ephesians 6:2,3

"As a boy grows, he begins to want not just external rules and laws but relationship with the father. 'Show us the Father,' as Philip asked Jesus, 'that is all we need' (John 14:8). For a teenager on the threshold of manhood, this translates 'Dad, I do appreciate the ways you've taught me right from wrong. But now, I want to

see you, the person: What was it like for you growing up? Did you get scared around girls? How do you like your job now? How do you and Mom get along?'
"And so when in our fear of punishment we had allowed the Law to replace relationship with the Father, God revealed himself personally in Jesus—who answers Philip, 'Whoever has seen me has seen the Father'" (John 14:9). [Gordon Dalbey, *Sons of the Father* (Wheaton, IL: Tyndale, 1992) p. 287.]

Key Ideas

God purposely designed men and women to bear children, and thus to keep the human race growing and expanding on the earth. Besides physical childbearing, men and women are also given the responsibility of feeding, clothing, sheltering, teaching and—most of all—loving their children. And God has instructed children to honor their parents. Although this can be challenging, because of the sinful and selfish nature of humans, it is the task of Christian young people to obey God's instruction, and to work toward an understanding and loving relationship with their parents—even the most difficult ones.

WARM UP

10 Minutes

- Show the video.

REMINDER: Inform students that handouts are not to be turned in. Discuss them, then they may keep or dispose of them.

10 Minutes

JACKIE'S STORY

- Share the following real-life story.

Jackie had just turned twelve when her parents told her they were getting a divorce. Jackie's father traveled a great deal, and for the past few years she hadn't seen him that often. For that reason, and because he was very critical when he was home, the divorce was not a huge problem for Jackie. What did become a problem for her, however, was the change that began to take place in Jackie's mother, Susan.

Susan was forty-two when she asked for the divorce and was still an attractive woman. For some reason, she began to attach herself to Jackie and her friends, hanging out with them, trying to include herself in their activities and starting to dress like them. At first, Jackie enjoyed having her mom around more and hoped that she and her friends were cheering her up during what was certainly a hard time in her life.

But, little by little, Jackie and her friends became uncomfortable with Susan's behavior. It was especially hard for Jackie when her mom added her own dating stories to the girls' conversations about their boyfriends. Jackie was incredibly embarrassed.

When Jackie tried to talk to her mother about her feelings, Susan became defensive and tearful. "I just want to be your friend!" she cried. "Most girls would be happy if their moms were young at heart and liked to go out with them. Most moms are old and critical and no fun. That's the way my mom was. Now that I'm single I want to have fun and I want for us to share the fun together!"

"I want to be friends too," Jackie explained. "But first of all I want you to be my mom. And I guess that means *act your age.*"

The conversation ended badly, with both Jackie and Susan in tears.

- Distribute "Jackie's Story" handout.
- Have students complete the page and discuss.
- After the discussion, conclude with the following: **Jackie's story is a true story, although her name has been changed to protect her identity. Here's what happened to Jackie.**

Jackie went to her church youth group on Thursday night. She asked to talk to the youth pastor's wife and poured out the whole story to her. They prayed together and asked God to give them both wisdom about the problem Jackie was having with her mom. Later on, when the youth pastor and his wife talked about it, they thought it might be helpful for Susan to meet some new friends through the church's singles group. They made some calls to trustworthy women in the singles group.

Susan received an invitation to a single's group dinner dance the following week. She went, and through the efforts of the Christian women who had become aware of her situation, she was befriended and invited to other functions. Gradually she got involved with single men and women her own age, and she became less and less dependent on Jackie and her friends for support.

TEAM EFFORT

15 Minutes

- Distribute "Dealing with Difficult Parents" handout.
- Divide students into three or more small groups.
- Assign each small group one of the three scenarios to discuss. If you have more than three groups, it's all right to assign the scenarios more than once.
- After about 10 minutes have each small group share their responses with the whole group

> **Note:** It is important to encourage participants to know that their conversations in this setting will be kept in strictest confidence—both by adult leaders and students. It would also be wise for you to find adult support (but not parents of the students) for the discussions this week. You might consider making arrangements in advance with qualified church members—preferably couples—who will step into any difficult situations that surface during the sessions. **If you haven't already done so, it might be a good time to introduce the Confidentiality Agreement.**

IN THE WORD

15 Minutes

Last week we looked at Joseph's godly behavior toward his family, even when they had treated him badly. This week, we are going to examine one of the psalms written by King David about the good things—both attitudes and actions—that Father God had shown him. Let's read Psalm 103.

- Have each student read one verse until all 22 verses have been read.

What are some of the things Father God has done for His son David? Make sure the following points are made:

- God forgave his sins and healed his diseases.
- God rescued him out of the pit, He surrounded him with love and tender mercies.

95

- He gives righteousness and justice to all who were treated unfairly.
- He is merciful and gracious; slow to get angry and full of unfailing love.
- God will not constantly accuse us, nor remain angry forever.
- God will not punish us for all our sins, nor deal with us as we deserve.
- My God understands how weak I am.

What are some of the wonderful promises Father God makes to us, if we are loyal to Him and do what He tells us to do? Make sure the following points are made:

- As high as the heavens are above the earth, so great is God's unfailing love.
- Father God is like a good earthly father who is tender and compassionate.
- God's love will remain forever.

Why do our earthly parents sometimes fail to be loving, kind and good?

How would you define "abuse" in relation to parents?

Why is it important for us to think of God as a Parent? As a Friend?

5 Minutes

Is it difficult for you to think of God as your Parent? As your Friend? Why? Why not?

Do you think having an unloving or abusive earthly father can make it difficult for us think of God as our heavenly Father or "Father God"?

- Distribute Father God handouts.

CLOSING PRAYER

Invite students to hold hands and to share with Father God their pain and disappointments. Pray that His presence will comfort each person there.

Jackie's Story

1. What was wrong with Susan's behavior?

2. What would you have done if you'd been in Jackie's situation?

3. What do you think caused Susan to behave the way she did?

4. What would you have told Jackie about her mom if you'd been one of her friends?

5. What does it mean for parents and their children to be friends?

What doesn't it mean?

Get all the advice and instruction you can, and be wise the rest of your life. **Proverbs 19:20**

Session 6

Dealing with Difficult Parents

We know that parents and children should be friends to one another, sharing love, respect, forgiveness, concern and support. Unfortunately, that is all too often an unrealistic scenario. Instead, kids have to figure out ways to cope with their difficult parents.

Scenario One: Your parents are chronic critics. They find fault with your thoughts, your actions, your looks and your friends. Even when you try to adjust yourself to please them, you can't win—something else is wrong. List some things you can do to live in peace with critical parents.

Scenario Two: Your parents are abusers—verbal, physical, emotional or sexual abusers. You are subjected to insults, degrading labels, physical attacks, violence or sexual abuse at the hands of one or both parents. What can you do in a case like this, and how can others help you?

Scenario Three: Because of unloving or neglectful parents, you find yourself *looking for love in all the wrong places.* You may be male- or female-dependent. You may be having a series of opposite sex or same-sex attractions or affairs. You may be struggling with terrible loneliness. Who can help you and how can you get help?

> *Turn to me and have mercy on me, for I am alone and in deep distress.* **Psalm 25:16**

Session 6

Making Friends with Your Parents

1. What are some of the positive attitudes you look for in a real friend?

2. What are some good things you'd expect to see a real friend do for you?

3. List some attitudes and actions that your parents would need to display so you could consider them to be your friends.

4. List some attitudes and actions that you would need to display for your parents to view you as their friend.

> *Grandchildren are the crowning glory of the aged; parents are the pride of their children.* **Proverbs 17:6**

Session 6

FATHER GOD

Father to the fatherless, defender of widows [abandoned ones]—this is God, whose dwelling is holy. Psalms 68:5

For the LORD hears the cries of his needy ones; he does not despise his people who are oppressed. Psalms 69:33

Sometimes your parents fall short of your expectations. They don't measure up to the examples you see in other, more desirable families. It could be that your parents' parents treated them in an unloving manner and they are only treating you like they were treated themselves.

With God's help you can forgive them, act differently yourself and break the cycle of abuse.

Father God knows what you go through and understands your feelings. He wants to be a very close friend, a parent to you. He will not bully His way into your life. Why don't you give Him a written invitation to come into Your life right now and become your closest Companion?

Dear Father God,

Love,
Your Adopted Child

Session 6

Absolutely Awful Attitudes

Is any one of you in trouble? He should pray. Is anyone happy? Let him sing songs of praise. Is any one of you sick? He should call the elders of the church to pray over him and anoint him with oil in the name of the Lord. And the prayer offered in faith will make the sick person well; the Lord will raise him up. If he has sinned, he will be forgiven. Therefore confess your sins to each other and pray for each other so that you may be healed. The prayer of a righteous man is powerful and effective . . . My brothers, if one of you should wander from the truth and someone should bring him back, remember this: Whoever turns a sinner from the error of his way will save him from death and cover over a multitude of sins. James 5:13-16,19,20 (NIV)

"Jesus was the kind of spiritual doctor who was willing to make house calls. He recognized the real world—a world of many great needs, the greatest being the need for salvation from sin.

"The fatal mistake of the Pharisees is still common today among evangelical Christians. We have mistakenly identified the unbeliever as the enemy rather than the victim of the enemy. We have erected unnecessary barriers between ourselves and the very ones we pray to reach. These barriers are usually cultural and not theological.

"We often communicate a legalistic attitude that says, 'If you practice certain activities you are not welcome in the Christian community.' Therefore, the non-believer receives an inflexible, judgmental attitude from the very ones who should be accepting him. The Christian community must keep the unbelievers' view of salvation uncluttered with cultural biases. We need to keep the message of salvation simple and pure, just as Jesus modeled it for us." [Bill Hull, *Jesus Christ Disciple-Maker* (Colorado Springs: Navpress, 1984) p. 101.]

Key Ideas

Because of sin in our world, we face all kinds of struggles, temptations and failures. Instead of looking at our own lives with attitudes of defeat and desperation, God wants us to turn to Him for answers. Instead of looking at others with bad attitudes of judgment or rejection, God wants us to reach out to others in their struggles.

WARM UP

10 Minutes

- Show the video.

> **REMINDER:** Inform students that handouts are not to be turned in. Discuss them, then they may keep or dispose of them.

REAL LIFE

10 Minutes

DOYLE'S STORY

- Share the following real-life story.

Doyle grew up in a blue-collar family—his father worked long hours at a factory near their home in Michigan, and his mother was a stay-at-home mom who spent most of her time taking care of her youngest child—a beautiful daughter who was her pride and joy. Doyle didn't get much attention from either parent and felt left out because his little sister seemed to be so much their parents' favorite. Doyle tried very hard to be perfect in everything he did, hoping to gain his parents' approval. But to Doyle, girls seemed better equipped to attract praise and applause. Gradually, he began to avoid rough sports, he hung out with girls and played girls' games. Doyle was soon labeled a "sissy" at school and before long the boys and teachers either ignored, avoided or rejected him.

At age 13, Doyle accepted Christ into his life, but other changes were taking place at the same time. He was ashamed of his feelings, but he was constantly attracted to other males. Doyle very carefully hid the same-sex adolescent crushes that often captured his imagination. During college after drinking excessively, Doyle had his first homosexual experiences, which he struggled to justify in light of his Christian faith. He was torn by the contradictions of his life—he wanted so much to be good, but he was constantly battling sexual and emotional urges that seemed to overpower him.

Fortunately, a godly young man named Joe became Doyle's roommate. Joe didn't have any understanding of homosexuality, but he could see that Doyle was struggling so he prayed with him. "Doyle," he said, "I don't have a clue about your problems, but God does. And I think He wants me to be your friend."

Doyle didn't avoid all the homosexual temptations that came his way during college. Sometimes he found himself feeling more than friendship toward some guys, and a few times he got tangled up in brief sexual relationships. But no matter what Doyle did, Joe continued to talk with him, encourage him in his Christian life, and pray with and for him.

For the first time in his life, Doyle felt accepted and unconditionally loved by another male. Then one day, during a campus praise and worship session, Doyle suddenly saw himself as a very small child, terrified and unable to respond to the outstretched arms of a male figure who was kneeling in front of him. He heard his own voice in his mind, saying *Daddy, I'm so scared!*

Doyle began to cry and fell to his knees. Seeing his deep pain, his Christian friends put their arms around him, held him and prayed with him. Because he was supported so firmly by other believers, at last Doyle could look at his needs for male acceptance in terms of his relationship with his earthly father.

- Distribute "Doyle's Story" handout.
- Have students complete the page and discuss.
- After the discussion, conclude with the following:

Doyle's story is a true story, although his name has been changed to protect his identity. Here's what happened to Doyle.

After acknowledging that his unloving relationship with his dad had caused him to feel drawn into same-sex relationships, Doyle was flooded with the love of Father God. He felt embraced and accepted by his heavenly Father. He sought Christian counseling to help him better understand his childhood experiences, and at last he was able to forgive his dad and be reconciled with him. Today Doyle is married, has three sons of his own and is involved in helping other people overcome their same-sex attractions through God's love and the support of fellow Christians.

TEAM EFFORT

15 Minutes

- Distribute "Really Awful Attitudes" handout.
- Have students complete the handout
- Have them form small groups of three to five and discuss the handout.

IN THE WORD

20 Minutes

Let's take a look at the lives of a trio of women in the Old Testament. In each case, their backgrounds and family histories were against them. Yet all three of them chose to go beyond their comfort zone, to pursue action steps toward positive change in their lives. In the New Testament, God honored all three of these women by naming them in the genealogy of His Son Jesus Christ.

RAHAB
Read Joshua 2:1-21; then summarize:

Rahab came from a promiscuous, pagan lifestyle, yet she risked her life and set herself up for ridicule by befriending and helping out strangers in their time of need.

RUTH
Summarize Ruth 1—4 :

Ruth's mother-in-law (Naomi) felt such pain following the deaths of her husband and two sons that she only allowed people to call her by the name "Mara" which means "bitter, sad in spirit." Ruth choose to be a loyal daughter-in-law to a bitter, broken woman even though it meant she had to live in a foreign country with people who were strangers to her.

TAMAR
Read Genesis 38; then summarize:

Tamar was greatly misunderstood and mistreated by her husband's family after his death, yet she chose to remain in the family. In a loving yet firm way she confronted the family patriarch. This resulted in forgiveness and reconciliation.

1. All three women faced potential rejection from family and/or peers for standing up for Father God's Law given in Deuteronomy 10:17-19:

> *The LORD your God is the God of gods and Lord of lords. He is the great God, mighty and awesome, who shows no partiality and takes no bribes. He gives justice to orphans and widows. He shows love to the foreigners living among you and gives them food and clothing. You, too, must show love to foreigners.*

2. Father God's New Testament Law—a warning against prejudice—is found in James 2:1:

> *"My dear brothers and sisters, how can you claim that you have faith in our glorious Lord Jesus Christ if you favor some people more than others?"*

- Distribute "Three Transformed Women" handout.
- Divide students into groups of three or four to discuss the handout.
- After assuring them that their comments will be kept in confidence, invite them to share their answers with the whole group.

FATHER GOD REFLECTION TIME

5 Minutes

Father God knows and understands what you are going through and He wants to comfort you. Are you willing to do the same—to extend His comfort to other people, even if they aren't especially lovable in your opinion?

When you see others hurting and/or facing peer rejection, Father God wants to stretch your comfort zone and He will enable you to take positive action steps to love and comfort them.

- Distribute Father God handouts.

CLOSING PRAYER

Invite students to join hands and share their struggles with bad attitudes with Father God. They may be uncomfortable talking aloud about their problems, in which case they should feel free to pray silently. Close by praying that the Lord will empower each person there to show unconditional love toward themselves and toward others.

Doyle's Story

1. What, in your opinion, was the biggest cause of Doyle's same-sex attractions?

2. Do you think Doyle's perfectionism made his same-sex struggle more challenging? Why or why not?

3. How do you think you would act toward Doyle (or, if you're a girl, toward a female with similar struggles) if he (or she) came into your life as a college roommate?

4. How important a part do you think Joe played in Doyle's life changes? Explain.

> "So now I am giving you a new commandment: Love each other. Just as I have loved you, you should love each other. Your love for one another will prove to the world that you are my disciples."
> John 13:34,35

Session 7

115

Really Awful Attitudes

1. Most teenagers struggle with intense emotions and find themselves really liking some people and really disliking others. On a bad day, what kinds of people really annoy you? Circle as many as you want.

Trendy people	Gothics	Other races/ethnics
Socially cool people	Overly-talkative people	Gay types
Jocks	Freaks	Religious fanatics
Nerds	Racists	Loudmouths
Druggies/stoners	Underachievers	Super shy people

Others _____

2. What bothers you most about the groups you circled?
   - ☐ I don't understand them.
   - ☐ I'm embarrassed by them.
   - ☐ I'm bored by them.
   - ☐ I don't want to be identified with them.
   - ☐ I can't explain it.
   - ☐ They make me sick.
   - ☐ All of the above
   - ☐ Other reason _____

3. What bothers you most about yourself?

4. Is it hard for you to love others with God's love? Explain.

> *Love each other intensely with all your hearts.* 1 Peter 1:22

Session 7

Three Transformed Women

Rahab, Ruth and Tamar had positive attitudes and took action steps to bring about change in their lives. What can we learn from them?

1. In what ways have you felt different than others because of your background or past experiences?

2. In your school or community, which people are being labeled and/or mistreated because they seem different?

3. Do you know someone that is hurting or feeling rejected because of homosexual tendencies? What kinds of things have happened to him or her?

4. What action step could you take that would give that person comfort or help him or her feel more accepted?

5. How would you describe your present attitude toward people who are different such as the ones you might have circled on the previous handout?

6. What can you do to bring about a positive change in your attitude?

I have determined to live by your laws. **Psalm 119:30**

Session 7

 FATHER GOD

Praise be to the God and Father of our Lord Jesus Christ, the Father of compassion and the God of all comfort, who comforts us in all our troubles, so that we can comfort those in any trouble with the comfort we ourselves have received from God. 2 Corinthians 1:3,4 (*NIV*)

Are you in need of God's special comfort today? Why not tell Father God about it?

Dear Father God,

Love,
Your Adopted Child

Do you know someone else who is hurting or feeling rejected? Ask Father God what He would like you to do for that hurting person.

Session 7

Which Is Worse?

"Do for others what you would like them to do for you. This is a summary of all that is taught in the law and the prophets." Matthew 7:12

"Too often Christians have failed to combine servanthood with truth. Too often we have been more ferocious in attacking sin than we are gentle in loving sinners. Too often our evangelism has come mixed with Western cultural arrogance . . . rather than immersed in acts of service and care. Too often our political engagement has been a self-serving demand for power rather than a servant voice for the poor and weak. Too often, we have failed to imitate our Servant King.

"Servanthood must be the hallmark of the Christian." [Ronald J. Sider, *Genuine Christianity: Essentials for Living Your Faith* (Grand Rapids: Zondervan, 1997) pp. 169, 176.]

Key Ideas

Homosexuality is a sin, according to God's Word, but many people are struggling with this issue and cannot be excluded from the company of Christians merely because they are confused about their sexuality.

WARM UP

10 Minutes

- Show the video.
- Distribute "From Bad to Worse" handout.
- Complete handout and discuss.
  Stress the fact that if we have broken any one of God's rules, we have broken them all. But God's grace is enough to cover all our sins, no matter how great or how small.

REMINDER: Inform students that handouts are not to be turned in. Discuss them, then they may keep or dispose of them.

TEAM EFFORT

15 Minutes

- Divide group in half. Distribute "Which Is Worse?" handout to one group and "Which Is the Worst Consequence?" handout to the other group. Have each group work together on their answers, and have them select a spokesperson to share their answers with the whole group.

- Discuss handouts with the whole group.

Wrap up the discussion by explaining: **It is important that we realize that people's personal preferences regarding sin and sin's consequences do not necessarily reflect biblical standards—sin is sin. The consequence of each behavior listed on "Which Is the Worst Consequence?" handout is—in the worst case scenario—death.**

IN THE WORD

15 Minutes

- Read Luke 15:11-32 aloud (or ask a volunteer to read).
- Then summarize as follows:

The familiar, yet amazing, story of the prodigal son, found in Luke 15:11-32, provides us with a living picture of Father God's love for a wayward child trapped in sin.

The son asked for his cut of his wealthy father's money. He then hit the road for a wild fling of extreme living. It didn't take long before he lost every dime, became destitute and longed to be back in his family's loving care. He made a dramatic turnaround. Regretting his sinful behavior, he humbly returned to his father and family, willing to at least live as his father's servant.

His father was watching for him. Seeing his lost son in the far distance, he ran toward him with open arms. The father's rejoicing was so intense that he threw a party for all the family's friends to rejoice with him in his newfound joy.

Only one person seemed to object—the prodigal's older brother was angry that his wayward brother was receiving so much attention. He complained that he had always been loyal to his father, and he engaged in a "pity party" for himself. The father reassured the older son of his love for him and of his appreciation for his long-term loyalty.

- Distribute "A Family Feud" handout.

- Either have students form groups of three or four to discuss, or discuss with the whole group.

- Conclude by discussing this question.

Who do you most identify with—the prodigal son or the elder brother? Why?

FATHER GOD REFLECTION TIME

5 Minutes

Have you received Father God s love gift, His Son Jesus?

Have you asked Him to come into your life as your personal Lord and Savior?

Have you thanked God for His love gift to you?

- Give students an opportunity to respond to these important questions.
- Distribute Father God handout.

CLOSING PRAYER

Invite students to join hands with one another and share with Father God their concerns about their own sins and failures, and their tendency to think of some sins as more sinful than others. Pray that His loving presence will be evident to each person present.

From Bad To Worse

Arrange the following sins in order from 1 to 10—with 10 being the most serious sin and 1 being the least serious sin.

___ lying
___ gossiping
___ cheating on a test
___ swearing
___ premarital sex
___ homosexuality
___ shoplifting
___ child abuse
___ sexual molestation
___ hating someone

1. Why do you think some people think one sin is the worst, and other people think a different sin is the worst?

2. Do you believe that God's grace is the same for all of us, no matter what we've done. Why or why not?

> God saved you by his special favor when you believed. And you can't take credit for this; it is a gift from God. Salvation is not a reward for the good things we have done, so none of us can boast about it. Ephesians 2:8,9

Session 8

Which Is Worse?

Scenario One: Bill and Joe are sixteen years old. They have discovered that they are both interested in homosexuality, and they are very emotionally attached to each other. After drinking too much at a party, they get involved in a homosexual sex act.

Scenario Two: Kevin and Jill are sophomores and they have been dating for two years. Their physical relationship has become more and more intense over the last few weeks. Jill's parents are gone for the weekend, and Jill and Kevin have the house to themselves. They have sexual intercourse for the first time.

Scenario Three: The Christian Center Youth Group has a visitor—Jesse, a young man of fifteen who has many characteristics that are identified as gay by other teenagers. The members of the youth group (especially the boys) take one look at Jesse and start making jokes among themselves. By the end of the meeting one of them tells Jesse, "This isn't a hangout for people like you. Go find some other place to look for faggots!"

Which of these scenarios is worse in God's eyes, and why?

Read the following Scripture passage; then apply it to the previous question.

If you really keep the royal law found in Scripture, "Love your neighbor as yourself," you are doing right. But if you show favoritism, you sin and are convicted by the law as lawbreakers. For whoever keeps the whole law and yet stumbles at just one point is guilty of breaking all of it. James 2:8-10 (*NIV*)

Get wisdom, get understanding. **Proverbs 4:5, *NIV***

Session 8

Which Is the Worst Consequence?

Scenario One: Bill and Joe are sixteen years old. They have discovered that they are both interested in homosexuality, and they are very emotionally attached to each other. After drinking too much at a party, they get involved in a homosexual sex act.

Scenario Two: Kevin and Jill are sophomores and they have been dating for two years. Their physical relationship has become more and more intense over the last few weeks. Jill's parents are gone for the weekend, and Jill and Kevin have the house to themselves. They have sexual intercourse for the first time.

Scenario Three: The Christian Center Youth Group has a visitor—Jesse, a young man of fifteen who has many characteristics that are identified as gay by other teenagers. The kids in the youth group (especially the boys) take one look at Jesse and start making jokes among themselves. By the end of the meeting one of them tells Jesse, "This isn't a hangout for people like you. Go find some other place to look for faggots!"

What do you think would be the worst possible consequence of each scenario?

1.

2.

3.

Read the following Scripture passage; then apply it to the previous question. *Do not be deceived: God cannot be mocked. A man reaps what he sows. The one who sows to please his sinful nature, from that nature will reap destruction; the one who sows to please the Spirit, from the Spirit will reap eternal life. (Galatians 6:7)*

Though it cost all you have, get understanding. **Proverbs 4:7, NIV**

Session 8

A Family Feud

The story of the prodigal son raises some interesting questions about truth and consequences. Mark what you think are the best answers to the following questions.

1. Why were the younger son's actions forgivable to the father?
   - ☐ His father was just a kind old man who had sadly missed his son; he didn't care what his son did or didn't do.
   - ☐ The father was getting old and senile.
   - ☐ The father had no idea what his son had been doing.
   - ☐ The father's love for his son was more powerful than his hatred of his son's sins.
   - ☐ Other _____

2. Was the older son out of line with his feelings of jealousy?
   - ☐ No, he simply wanted equal treatment for his long-term loyalty.
   - ☐ Yes, his brother's changed life should have caused him to be happy.
   - ☐ Yes, he was really very insensitive to the rejoicing of his father.
   - ☐ No, anyone doing those reckless detestable things should not be given a second chance.
   - ☐ Other _____

3. Explain how the elder brother's attitude might be compared with some Christian's attitudes toward God when He forgives homosexuals.

4. What do you learn about Father God's love from this story?

> "So now I am giving you a new commandment: Love each other. Just as I have loved you, you should love each other. Your love for one another will prove to the world that you are my disciples."
> John 13:34,35

Session 8

 FATHER GOD

"For God so loved the world that he gave his only Son, so that everyone who believes in him will not perish but have eternal life. God did not send his Son into the world to condemn it, but to save it." John 3:16,17

Father God longs for His wayward sons and daughters to return to Him. In fact, the only condition of our welcome is that we choose to accept Jesus and receive the free gift of forgiveness that Father God offers us through Him.

What would you like to say to Father God about His love, His Son's death and His offer of salvation?

Dear Father God,

Love,
Your Adopted Child

Pressing On

No, dear brothers and sisters, I am still not all I should be, but I am focusing all my energies on this one thing: Forgetting the past and looking forward to what lies ahead, I strain to reach the end of the race and receive the prize for which God, through Christ Jesus, is calling us up to heaven. Philippians 3:13,14

"The road ahead will take us into a deepening and a focusing of our desire. As author James Houston has experienced, 'The desire that really gives life is to know God. This desire is never satisfied, for it is one that grows with its fulfillment; and our relationship with God changes and leads to a constant deepening of our desires.'" [Brent Curtis and John Eldredge, *The Sacred Romance: Drawing Closer to the Heart of God* (Nashville: Thomas Nelson Publishers, 1997) p. 200.]

Key Ideas

When we try to change ourselves, we usually fail. And even when God changes us, it rarely happens instantly, but it is typically a process. That's why we need to be patient and forgiving of both ourselves and of others, and we should support one another emotionally and spiritually as God changes our hearts and makes us new.

WARM UP

10 Minutes

- Play the Coral Ridge video
- Invite students to react to the video.

> **REMINDER:** Inform students that handouts are not to be turned in. Discuss them, then they may keep or dispose of them.

REAL LIFE

10 Minutes

KIM AND SAM'S STORY

- Share this real-life story.

Kim was the president of the high school Sunday School class at her church, and she made it a point to try to befriend every new student who attended the group. When Sam arrived with his red mohawk, green fingernails and bizarre stories about sexual experimentation of every kind, most of the kids in the group recoiled. But Kim was, as usual, friendly and considerate. She spent a lot of time talking to Sam after the first meeting, called him during the week and met him for coffee on Saturday afternoon. Her goal was to encourage him to come back to church the next week.

Kim's mother got a phone call from a concerned friend, informing her that Kim was at Starbuck's with a freaky-looking boy. She was waiting to confront Kim by the time she got home.

"I just want to lead him to the Lord," Kim explained. "He's so confused. He's really not a bad kid."

"I know what he's like. Everyone knows he's bisexual and a druggie, not to mention his personal appearance! How can you do this to us? You'll ruin your Christian testimony, and he'll drag you down with him. And what about our family? Your father is an elder at the church!"

Kim looked at her mother sadly. She longed to share with her what she and Sam had talked about, but knew better than to try.

The next day, when Sam arrived at church, at Kim's insistence several of the kids talked to him and made a point of inviting him to a beach party the following week.

Meanwhile Kim's mother went to the pastor and complained about Sam's attendance at the church. "He's satanic. Can't you tell by looking at him? He's a pervert who has actually told people that he's bisexual. I want you to fire the youth director if he doesn't kick this kid out!"

The pastor looked at Kim's mother sadly. "Do you think Jesus would kick him out?" he asked. "I think Jesus was the Son of God and that He could deal with anyone. These kids are young, naïve and weak. They shouldn't be exposed to this kind of thing."

Kim's mother left the pastor's office in an angry mood, and Kim got the full brunt of it that night: "If that boy is going to the beach party on Saturday, you aren't! And that's final!"

"Look, I don't know if he's going or not, Mom," Kim said as calmly as possible. "But if he does, I promise not to hang out with him, okay? I have to go to the party because I'm the class president. Why can't you trust me, anyway? Have I given you any reason not to?"

"Going out with a boy like that is plenty of reason!" Kim's mother shouted, storming out of the room and slamming the door behind her.

- Distribute "Kim and Sam's Story" handout.
- Have students complete the page and discuss.
- Conclude the discussion with the following explanation:

Sam and Kim's story is a true story, although their names have been changed to protect their identities. Here's what happened to Sam and Kim.

Sam went to the beach party. Beforehand, Kim had talked to several of the boys in the group and asked them to include Sam in their activities instead of leaving Kim to deal with him on her own. She knew from her conversations with Sam that he was very close to accepting Christ into his life. "He needs to connect with you guys, so he'll have some Christian males in his life, too," she explained.

At the end of the beach party, after singing songs around a campfire and listening to a short Bible study, the youth director asked if any of the kids wanted to receive Christ. Sam immediately raised his hand. Over the course of the following year, Sam began to change. Little by little, his looks, his speech and his attitude were completely transformed. His red mohawk was gone; his fingernails were no longer fluorescent green.

One day Sam approached Kim's mother and told her that he was now a Christian. "Your daughter made a huge difference in my life," he explained. "And I want to thank you for your patience with me during the process."

Kim's mother was both shocked and ashamed. She didn't exactly apologize to Kim when she got home, but she did tell her what Sam had said and that she was proud of her.

"Thanks, Lord," Kim prayed silently as she went to her room. "That's more than I expected from her."

TEAM EFFORT

15 Minutes

- Distribute "Dealing with Different People" handout.
- Invite students to complete the first two questions alone.
- Then have students form groups of three to five and discuss the rest of the handout.

Stress the possibility of change in their lives and the fact that God wants to change all of us through His Holy Spirit.

IN THE WORD

15 Minutes

We can learn a great deal about how Jesus related to socially unacceptable people by reading the story of the woman at the well in John 4:3-42. Let's read the story, and then take a brief look at it, along with some cultural background that lay behind it.

Jews and Samaritans are distant relatives, and in Jesus' time, they had allowed some hard racial barriers to develop between them. Not only were they not on speaking terms, but the Jews wouldn't so much as cross the boundaries of the Samaritan community when traveling, even if it meant taking a much longer route walking around Samaria.

In this story, Jesus defied the laws of tradition and broke through racial barriers by going into Samaria intentionally. Once he was there, he asked a favor of a woman: Would she please give him a drink?

That might not seem so bad, except the Jews traditionally would not speak to a despised Samaritan. In fact, traditionally Jewish men would never speak to a woman who was not a relative, much less ask a favor of her.

Instead of abiding by these manmade laws, Jesus paid the woman a very big compliment by talking to her. This really caught her off guard. He revealed the truth about Father God to her as he answered her questions. He also brought to the surface her questionable lifestyle—she had been married several times, and was now living with a man to whom she wasn't married.

Amazed by His extraordinary knowledge, the woman asked, "Are you a prophet? Are you the Messiah who's coming from Father God?"

"Yes," Jesus answered.

The woman was so excited that she ran through her village announcing who Jesus was and declaring her belief in Him. Many in the town came and also believed in Jesus because of what they had heard from the woman. Because of her, they were able to meet Jesus themselves.

- Distribute "The Woman at the Well" handout.
- Have students discuss the handout in their small groups and then share their answers with the whole group.

FATHER GOD REFLECTION TIME

5 Minutes

Since Father God already sees you as complete and perfect, as if you were Jesus, His beloved Son, how does this affect you in your efforts to change your behavior?

How can you better share Father God's unconditional love with those who are hurting?

- Distribute Father God handouts.

CLOSING PRAYER

Invite students to join hands and share with Father God their struggles and their own desire for change. Pray that He will empower each person present to show unconditional love toward themselves and others, no matter what their struggles.

Kim And Sam's Story

1. Why do you think people like Sam choose to look outrageous?

2. Do you find it easy or hard to relate to people who have numerous tattoos, multiple piercings, punk-style hair or claim to be sexually adventurous? Explain.

3. Did Kim's mother have a valid point in her concern, or was she completely out of line? Explain.

4. How would you and your friends respond to Sam if he showed up at your church?

5. Describe how you think Jesus would treat Sam.

6. Do you believe people can really change? Explain.

"Healthy people don't need a doctor—sick people do." Matthew 9:12

Session 9

Dealing with Different People

1. Sometime people choose styles, mannerisms and language in order to hide their feelings of fear, possible rejection or social discomfort. Psychologists call these forms of self-protection "defense mechanisms." Circle the defense mechanisms you may have used at one time or another.

Bragging	Criticizing others	Using bad language
Making fun of people	Being loud	Gossiping
Showing off	Refusing to participate	Driving too fast
Wearing trendy clothes	Being in a clique	Using drugs or alcohol
Being controlling	Being quiet or shy	Being competitive

2. Have you changed? How do you feel now about the defense mechanisms you used before and the way you used to act?

3. What might be some of your reasons for avoiding weird people like Sam?
   - ☐ They scare me.
   - ☐ I don't like the idea of bisexuality.
   - ☐ I don't want to be seen with them.
   - ☐ I'm afraid I'll get AIDS or some other disease.
   - ☐ They are probably crazy and I don't want to get involved with crazies.
   - ☐ I have enough problems of my own.
   - ☐ I don't want people to think Christians hang out with people like that.
   - ☐ My parents would kill me.

4. How can a Christian youth group bring about change in the lives of troubled kids without allowing them to have a negative influence on the members of the group?

> *We are therefore Christ's ambassadors, as though God were making his appeal through us. 2 Corinthians 5:20, NIV*

Session 9

The Woman at the Well

Jesus broke several taboos of His day by befriending and speaking honorably with a despised woman who had a questionable background.

1. Are there social taboos in your circle of Christian friends that might cause you or them to shy away from showing a genuine interest in certain people? List a few of those taboos:

2. What is the best way to be a friend to someone who, for some reason, is rejected by others?

3. Can you think of someone who demonstrates homosexual mannerisms or claims to be gay? Without naming names, explain your feelings about this person.

4. Do you think Jesus would have treated the woman of Samaria differently if she had been involved in homosexual behavior? Explain.

Those who listen to my message and believe in God who sent me have eternal life and will never be condemned for their sins. **John 5:24**

Session 9

 FATHER GOD

For every one of you are mature sons of God through faith in Christ Jesus. For you were immersed into Christ. We have clothed ourselves with Christ. Galatians 3:27, *NIV*

Did you know that whenever God looks at you—if you are a believer—He sees *Jesus*? He sees His mature, godly, perfect Son. So every time He sees you, He smiles. Every time He sees you, He feels good. He sees and understands you more deeply than even your family does. He sees you totally "immersed into Christ." He identifies you with His beloved Son, Jesus Christ.

How has your family influenced the way you see yourself? Tell Father God about it.

Dear Father God,

Love,
Your Adopted Child

Lean On Me

Share each other's troubles and problems, and in this way obey the law of Christ. Galatians 6:2

"Jesus Christ is the wounded Healer. He knows how our emotions can be injured. Indeed, He was tempted in every way that we have been tempted.

"His very birth was questioned, and His mother's reputation was slandered. He was born in poverty. His race was ostracized and His hometown ridiculed. His father died when He was young and in His latter years Jesus traveled the streets and cities homeless. He was misunderstood in His ministry, and abandoned in death. He did all this for you and me. He did it to identify with us in weakness: 'We have not a high priest who is unable to sympathize with our weaknesses, but one who in every respect has been tempted as we are, yet without sin. Let us then with confidence draw near to the throne of grace, that we may receive mercy and find grace to help in time of need' (Hebrews 4:15-16)." [Floyd McClung, Jr., *The Father Heart of God* (Eugene, OR: Harvest House, 1985) pp. 40,41.]

Key Ideas

When we try to change ourselves, we usually fail. And even when God changes us, it rarely happens instantly, but it is typically a process. That's why we need to be patient and forgiving of both ourselves and of others, and we should support one another emotionally and spiritually as God changes our hearts and makes us new.

WARM UP

10 Minutes

- Show the video.

> **REMINDER:** Inform students that handouts are not to be turned in. Discuss them, then they may keep or dispose of them.

REAL LIFE

10 Minutes

RON'S STORY

- Share the following real-life story:

  Ron was seventeen when he first learned that his mother was seriously ill. His father and his uncle took him aside and explained that she had cancer, and wasn't likely to live more than a few months. Ron's dad had recently divorced his mom, and Ron still lived with her, so he felt especially vulnerable because he had no idea what would happen to him once she died. Ron felt very disconnected from his father, and his

mother was the only person on earth who seemed to really love him. Now, suddenly Ron was faced with the possibility of losing her, and the situation was so painful and frightening to him that he simply couldn't talk about it. Ron's dad, who lived on the other side of the country with his new wife, never mentioned her illness on his rare phone calls to his son. And his mother simply avoided the subject of her health altogether.

Months passed, and although by now she was wearing a wig and had become very thin, Ron thought his mother seemed more or less all right. Sometimes she went to the hospital for a few days, but she was very matter of fact about it, and Ron simply took care of himself until she got back.

During one of her hospital stays, Ron got a call from his mother's doctor. "You'd better get over here," he said, his voice worried and tense. "I don't know how long she has."

Ron jumped in the car and drove over to the hospital in a daze. By the time he got there, his mother was unconscious. Within an hour, she was gone and he never got the opportunity to say goodbye to her.

Ron's aunts planned the funeral, which was held at a local church. Ron had been there a few times in his life, but he hadn't been back for several months. After the services, the pastor took Ron aside and talked to him.

"This has got to be a terrible heartache for you, Ron." he said. "How are you doing?"

Ron had almost no expression on his face. "I'm fine," he said in a monotone voice. "I'll be fine."

"Where are you planning to live?"

"What do you mean?"

"Well, with your Mom gone, you can't really keep living at your house alone—"

"I'll talk to my dad. He's coming to see me next week. We'll figure something out."

"Do you have some friends to talk to?"

"I'm fine," Ron repeated, looking around nervously and excusing himself from the conversation.

- Distribute "Ron's Story" handout.
- Have students complete the page and discuss.
- After the discussion, conclude with the following:

Ron's story is a true story, although his name has been changed to protect his identity. Here's what happened to Ron.

The pastor got Ron's father's phone number from some relatives at the funeral. He called and tried to talk to him, but Ron's dad was rather rude and noncommittal. "He's an adult, you know," he told the pastor. "Let him find his own way. It'll make a man out of him."

The pastor and the church's youth pastor prayed together, asking the Lord for direction. Together they went to see Ron's high school counselor and his academic advisor. They, along with his aunt, worked out a plan for Ron to stay with one of the church families until time for him to go to college.

At first Ron refused to leave his house. He seemed completely unable to face the reality of what had happened. After a few days, though, after realizing that the house was about to be sold, he reluctantly agreed that he would be able to live more comfortably in a family environment.

But for weeks, he refused to discuss his mother's death, his parent's divorce or his father's new marriage. Only through prayer, patience and a pattern of ongoing kindness did Ron learn to trust his new family. Eventually, because of the family's unconditional love for him, Ron also came to trust Christ.

15 Minutes	### TEAM EFFORT

- Distribute "Finding and Being a Friend" handout.
- Have students form groups of three or four and discuss the rankings they gave the attributes of a friend.

Point out the importance of finding trustworthy friends and of being a trustworthy confidante. Also, discuss when adult help should be sought and who would be appropriate adults to go to for help.

IN THE WORD

15 Minutes

- Read the following Scripture passages and then share the information that follows:

> *Then Jesus said, "Come to me, all of you who are weary and carry heavy burdens, and I will give you rest. Take my yoke upon you. Let me teach you, because I am humble and gentle, and you will find rest for your souls. For my yoke fits perfectly, and the burden I give you is light."* **Matthew 11:28-30**
>
> *"Give all your worries and cares to God, for he cares about what happens to you."*
> **1 Peter 5:7**

God's Word makes it clear to us that He wants to be involved in every aspect of our lives. Sometimes it is hard for us to believe that God really cares about our everyday lives. Other times, we think our stuff isn't worthy of God's time: I don't want to bother talking to God about things I can handle myself. Or we get the idea that He's kind of mad at us and that's why we have problems, so why bother talking to Him?

The reality is that God loves us unconditionally, and He wants us to talk to Him no matter what we may have done to offend Him. Father God is big enough to know every detail of our lives, and as Jesus said, even to the number of hairs on our heads (see Luke 12:6,7). Turning to Him, trusting Him and relying on Him is the most effective way to remove stress, anxiety and fear from our lives.

But God often works through people. In fact, His Word reminds us that as His people we reveal God's love to the world. When we turn to God, we will probably be led to seek out others who will walk with us—we will bear their burdens and they will bear ours.

We may also find that He places specific people in our lives to help us bear our burdens.

- Distribute "Leaning on the Lord" handout.
- Have students discuss questions 1 to 3 in their small groups.
- Invite them to share their answers with the whole group.
- Set aside a minute or two for students to answer question 4 on their own.

FATHER GOD REFLECTION TIME

5 Minutes

- Distribute Father God handout.

CLOSING PRAYER

Lead students in prayer time about their friends and friendships.

Ron's Story

1. Why do you think it was so difficult for Ron to talk about his situation?

2. Are some people more comfortable talking about their personal lives than other people? Are girls more comfortable than boys? Explain.

3. How did Ron's mother's reaction to her illness affect Ron's reaction?

4. How did Ron's father's situation affect Ron's reaction?

5. What might you have done if you'd found out about Ron's situation before his mother died? After she died?

> *Even if my father and mother abandon me, the LORD will hold me close.* **Psalm 27:10**

Session 10

Finding And Being A Good Friend

IF YOU NEED A FRIEND

There are some important things to keep in mind when you're looking for someone you can confide in. After each characteristic, write the names of three people in your life who best fit it:

Humble   _____ _____ _____

Uncritical   _____ _____ _____

Kind   _____ _____ _____

Honest   _____ _____ _____

Trustworthy   _____ _____ _____

Positive   _____ _____ _____

Available   _____ _____ _____

Not a hypocrite _____ _____ _____

No personal agenda _____ _____ _____

After filling out three names for each section, whose name did you write most often? The person I know with the most attributes of a good confidante is _____.

IF YOU WANT TO BE A FRIEND

What qualities makes a person a good friend? Number the following (from 1 to 11) in what you believe to be their order of importance.

__ Good listener
__ Understands you
__ Doesn't gossip
__ Loves God
__ Doesn't pass judgment
__ Will tell you the truth
__ Likes to have fun

__ Has the same values as you
__ Is loyal and trustworthy
__ Doesn't make fun of other people
__ Shares your taste in music and movies
__ Has a good sense of humor

A gossip tells secrets, so don't hang around with someone who talks too much. **Proverbs 20:19**

Session 10

Leaning on the Lord

1. When you hear the statement "Give all your worries and cares to God," what does that mean to you?

2. How can you give your anxiety to God?

3. What's your honest reaction when you hear this statement: "Jesus, God's Son, offers rest from inner turmoil and outside pressures"?

   ☐ It's too good to be true—even unbelievable.
   ☐ It's true if you're doing everything right so that God is happy with you.
   ☐ It's only true about spiritual needs—doesn't apply to everyday problems with parents, friends, mistakes or emotions.
   ☐ It's true for those who are serious about getting to know Jesus better.
   ☐ It's only available to those who prove themselves worthy for a year or more.

4. After reading the following Scripture passage, turn the paper over and write what Christ's death on the cross means to you personally.

> *But God showed his great love for us by sending Christ to die for us while we were still sinners. And since we have been made right in God's sight by the blood of Christ, he will certainly save us from God's judgment. For since we were restored to friendship with God by the death of his Son while we were still his enemies, we will certainly be delivered from eternal punishment by his life. So now we can rejoice in our wonderful new relationship with God—all because of what our Lord Jesus Christ has done for us in making us friends of God.* Romans 5:8-11

Session 10

 FATHER GOD

The apostle Paul wrote: *"And I am convinced that nothing can ever separate us from his love. Death can't, and life can't. The angels can't, and the demons can't. Our fears for today, our worries about tomorrow, and even the powers of hell can't keep God's love away. Whether we are high above the sky or in the deepest ocean, nothing in all creation will ever be able to separate us from the love of God that is revealed in Christ Jesus our Lord."* Romans 8:38,39

Much of the good we experience in life today seems to happen to us on a conditional basis so that we might think that . . .

Friends like me if . . .
Parents only seem to pay attention to me when. . .
My future will be bright only if. . .
I am a valuable person when. . .

Thankfully, Father God loves every person unconditionally. He has demonstrated His unconditional love through the death and resurrection of His Son Jesus for you.

How would you describe to God your feelings about being loved unconditionally?

Dear Father God,

Love,
Your Adopted Child

Forgiving the Unforgiveable

Key Verses

If you forgive those who sin against you, your heavenly Father will forgive you. But if you refuse to forgive others, your Father will not forgive your sins. Matthew 6:14,15

For God is working in you, giving you the desire to obey him and the power to do what pleases him. Philippians 2:13

Notable Quote

"People have many times come to us saying 'Don't talk to me about a loving God. Why doesn't he stop all the wars, or at least prevent some of the bestial things men do to men, sometimes in the very name of religion . . . We ask, 'What was your father like?' Invariably we uncover a history similar to what the counselee has imputed to God—cruelty, insensitivity, desertion, criticism, etc. No matter what the mind may learn in Sunday school of a gentle and loving God . . . the heart has been scarred and shaped by reactions to the earthly father, and projects that onto God. Not until such people forgive their natural fathers can they in fact see God as gentle and kind and lovingly present for them." [John and Paula Sandford, quoted in Gordon Dalbey, *Sons of the Father* (Wheaton: Tyndale House, 1992) p. 35.]

Key Ideas

Forgiveness is what makes our relationship with God possible—He has forgiven all our sins so that He can freely love us and be in relationship with us. In response to His forgiveness of us, He expects us to forgive one another.

WARM UP

10 Minutes

- Show the video.

REMINDER: Inform students that handouts are not to be turned in. Discuss them, then they may keep or dispose of them.

REAL LIFE

10 Minutes

CHELSEA'S STORY

- Share the following real-life story:

Chelsea hated her mother and stepfather. She hated their looks, their clothes, their favorite foods, their boring conversations and their loudmouthed friends. Most of all, she hated the times when they tried to include her in their lives. She didn't want to be with them, and she did all kinds of things to make them feel ashamed to be seen with her. She dyed her hair green. She pierced her nose and double pierced her left eyebrow. She got a tattoo on her hand. And she often got into loud, angry arguments with her mother in public.

For the most part, her strategy worked. Her parents stopped trying to spend time with her. But it didn't remove the hate from her heart. "They are so disgusting!" she would tell her friends. "You just don't know how stupid they are!"

Meanwhile, through some friends at school, Chelsea became intrigued with Jesus Christ. She started asking her Christian friends questions about faith, eternity and God's plan for each person's life. Chelsea became more and more interested, and eventually she prayed with one of her friends, asking Jesus to forgive her sins and to come into her life.

One night, during a Christian meeting, the subject of parents came up. Chelsea quickly told the group what she thought about hers. "I hate them so much. I wish I could disown them and go live with someone else. I really mean it!" Kathleen, the group leader, listened to Chelsea's outburst quietly and then asked, "What did your mother and stepfather do to make you hate them so much, Chelsea?"

Chelsea looked at her blankly. "What do you mean? It's not what they did, it's what they are. They are just complete idiots!"

Kathleen shook her head. "No, I think there's more to it than that, Chelsea. How long has your stepfather been in your life?"

"I don't know what you're talking about, Kathleen. But to answer your question, he's been around for three years."

"And do you still see your father?"

Chelsea looked at Kathleen suspiciously.

"What are you getting at?"

"Chelsea, I think you hate your mother and stepfather, at least in part, because your family isn't the way it used to be. Isn't that true?"

Chelsea tried to answer, but instead she began to cry. "I don't want to talk about it."

Kathleen called Chelsea up a few days later and invited her to go out to dinner. She explained that she wanted to talk to her some more.

"I don't want to talk about all that past stuff," Chelsea warned.

"That's fine. I want to talk to you about something else—about forgiveness."

At dinner, Kathleen explained to Chelsea that, as a new Christian, she had much to be thankful for. God had forgiven all her sins, past, present and future. And He had welcomed her into His family with open arms. "But He expects you to forgive others just as He's forgiven you. And that includes your parents, Chelsea."

"What makes you think I need to forgive them?"

"Aren't you still angry about the divorce and your mother's remarriage?"

"Wouldn't you be?" Chelsea spat out. "She had an affair and dumped my father for that jerk she's married to. And now I'll probably never see my father again! Wouldn't you be angry?"

Kathleen nodded. "I'd be very angry, Chelsea. But as a Christian, I'd still have to obey God and forgive them."

Chelsea was crying again. "I can't do that! It's just too much to ask."

"Why don't you just do this much—tell God you're willing to obey Him, even though you don't feel like it right now. Then ask Him to help you. Leave the rest to Him."

- Distribute "Chelsea's Story" handout.
- Have students complete the page and discuss.
- Conclude with the following:

Chelsea's story is a true story, although her name has been changed to protect her identity. Here's what happened to Chelsea.

It wasn't easy. Chelsea was embittered toward her mother for cheating on her dad, and blamed her stepfather for her mother's unfaithfulness. But after several weeks of prayer and Christian counsel, Chelsea was actually able to forgive her mother and stepfather for the affair they'd had that had led to the divorce.

Chelsea was finally able to tell her mother about her anger, and Chelsea's mother actually asked Chelsea to forgive her. Then she suggested that Chelsea write to her father and ask him to be more involved in her life. Chelsea learned that in her father's pain, he had simply left her behind, assuming that she didn't love him. She has since been reconciled with her father, and over a year's time, she has gradually learned to respect and care for her stepfather as well.

TEAM EFFORT

20 Minutes

- Distribute "A Closer Look at Forgiveness" handout.
- Have students form groups of three to five to discuss the questions.
- Have groups share their answers. Be sure to make the point that for Christians, forgiveness is not an option—it is a requirement.

IN THE WORD

15 Minutes

In Matthew 18:21-35, Jesus was asked how many times each of us should forgive another person. The following is a brief description of His answer.

Jesus explained that the kingdom of heaven can be compared to a king who loaned millions of dollars to one of his subjects. When the account came due and the man couldn't come up with the money, he begged the king for patience in repaying the loan. In a surprise move, the king showed pity to the man, released him and forgave his debt completely.

But after being forgiven of his debt, that same man went after some poor guy who owed him a $100. He refused to listen to his debtor's pleas for mercy. Instead, he had the man thrown in jail as punishment for his unpaid $100 loan.

The king heard about what had happened and he couldn't understand how the same man he'd forgiven had treated someone else so badly. He called him into his presence and said, "Shouldn't you have mercy on your fellow servant, just as I had mercy on you?"

The king then threw the man into prison until he could pay the original million dollar debt.

Jesus concluded His story by saying, "That's what my heavenly Father will do to you if you refuse to forgive your brothers and sisters in your heart."

Jesus also had some other points to make about offenses, grudges and forgiveness.

If you have sinned against another, and you recall this sin when you are about to offer a gift to God, Jesus says that you need to clear up the offense before you give God your gift." (Matthew 5:23,24, paraphrased)

Jesus said, "If a fellow believer has sinned against you, you first need to go by yourself to that person and talk to him about what happened. If that is unacceptable to him, then take another person with you. If your effort to settle the issue is still unacceptable to him, then take it before the church body." (Matthew 18:15-17, paraphrased)

No matter what happens, who does Jesus hold responsible to begin the forgiveness process?

a. The person who did the injustice toward me.
b. My friend, who knows the truth about what happened.
c. Me, it's always my move to see that the forgiveness process takes place.

C is the answer. Yes, it's always up to us.

- Distribute "Forgiveness—No Matter What" handout.
- Have students discuss the questions in small groups or with the whole group.

FATHER GOD REFLECTION TIME

5 Minutes

Explain: **Through forgiveness, Father God has completely changed the course of our destiny. He couldn't look on our sin, which meant we were banished from His presence eternally. But when Jesus died in our place, He made it possible for all our sin to be forgiven and removed from our record so we can be His adopted daughters and sons. None of this could have happened if Jesus hadn't died for us and risen from the grave and if Father God hadn't forgiven us.**

- Distribute Father God handout.

CLOSING PRAYER

Ask students to form small groups. Encourage them to silently ask God to reveal to them hidden grudges (they shouldn't talk about their specific grudges out loud), then to pray for one another to find courage to face their hurts and to seek God's help in forgiving others, even when it seems too hard.

Chelsea's Story

1. What, in your opinion, was Chelsea's biggest problem? Check one.
   - ☐ Disgust over her mother's sin
   - ☐ Anger at feeling left out
   - ☐ Hurt over the loss of her family life
   - ☐ Embarrassment over her mother and stepfather
   - ☐ Weird taste in hair color and other trends
   - ☐ Missing her father

2. How can unforgiveness lead to anger and rebellion?

3. Do you think Chelsea really hated her mother and stepfather? Explain.

4. Forgiveness seems to be harder for some people than for others. Is forgiveness hard or easy for you? Explain.

> *Forgive us our sins, just as we have forgiven those who have sinned against us.* Matthew 6:12

Session 11

173

A Closer Look at Forgiveness

1. In your opinion what, if anything, is unforgivable? Explain.

2. To understand forgiveness, sometimes we have to think about what forgiveness is not. Check the items that, in your opinion, are not part of forgiveness.

☐ Trusting   ☐ Letting go of bad feelings
☐ Saying "it didn't matter"   ☐ Blaming yourself
☐ Forgetting   ☐ Acting like it never happened
☐ Pretending you're not hurt   ☐ Smile now, get even later

3. It is sometimes said that the door to forgiveness is opened with three keys.

Key One: I can't. My heart is too bitter and I'm too hurt.
Key Two: God can. Jesus forgave those who killed Him.
Key Three: I'll let Him. He will help me forgive if I let Him do it through me.

Do these three keys make sense to you? Why or why not?

> *Love your enemies. Do good to those who hate you. Pray for the happiness of those who curse you. Pray for those who hurt you.* **Luke 6:27,28.**

Session 11

Forgiveness - No Matter What

1. Suppose you are the king in the story. You have forgiven one of your subjects a very large amount of money (or maybe a huge injustice done to you). How do you feel when you see that same person refusing to forgive someone else's very small injustice?

2. Is forgiving someone your own age easier or harder for you than forgiving an adult? Explain.

3. Sometimes terrible things happen, and we have to forgive such things as abandonment, betrayal, murder, sexual or physical abuse. How would you advise a friend to begin the process of forgiveness in such an extreme case?

> *Be kind to each other, tenderhearted, forgiving one another, just as God through Christ has forgiven you. Ephesians 4:32*

Session 11

FATHER GOD

Furthermore, because of Christ, we have received an inheritance from God, for he chose us from the beginning, and all things happen just as he decided long ago. God's purpose was that we who were the first to trust in Christ should praise our glorious God. And now you also have heard the truth, the Good News that God saves you. And when you believed in Christ, he identified you as his own by giving you the Holy Spirit, whom he promised long ago. The Spirit is God's guarantee that he will give us everything he promised and that he has purchased us to be his own people. This is just one more reason for us to praise our glorious God.
Ephesians 1:11-14

When you place your trust in Jesus, Father God...

- **Makes you an heir to eternal treasures through Jesus.**
- **Identifies you as His very own child.**
- **Gives His Holy Spirit to you: to teach you, to comfort you, to help you grow spiritually and to give you peace.**

Think about each of these gifts and try to describe what they mean to you.

Dear Father God,

Love,
Your Adopted Child

Reparenting with Father God

Even if my father and mother abandon me, the LORD will hold me close. Psalm 27:10 (paraphrased)

But when the time had fully come, God sent his Son, born of a woman, born under the law, to buy freedom for those under law, so that he could adopt us as his very own children. Because you are sons, God sent the Spirit of his Son into your hearts, and now you can call God your dear Father. So you are no longer an outcast but his own child. And since you are his child, everything he has belongs to you. Galatians 4:4-7 (paraphrased)

"God is not, as Freud once scoffed, simply 'a father substitute,' but the true Father we long for. We forget this when we naturally make the earthly father a God substitute. To see God accurately, a man must see his father

181

accurately—for better or for worse. But in order to let go of Dad as a saving idol—to see Dad as human and God as the true Father—a man must become human enough to remember his own sinful condition and the Father who has come in Jesus to save him from its deadly effects." [Gordon Dalbey, *Sons of the Father* (Wheaton: Tyndale House, 1992) p. 287.]

Key Ideas

God is our ultimate parent, with the aspects and attributes of both a perfect father *and* a perfect mother. He is able to love us, care for us, guide us and teach us. If we ask Him, God is willing to step in and reparent us in all the ways our earthly parents may have failed us.

WARM UP

10 Minutes

- Show the video.

REMINDER: Inform students that handouts are not to be turned in. Discuss them, then they may keep or dispose of them.

REAL LIFE

15 Minutes

UNDERSTANDING OUR OWN STORIES

- Invite students to share ideas about the qualities of good earthly parents.

The following are qualities that you'll want to introduce if they don't. Good parents:

- Are unconditionally loving/loyal/affirming
- Provide discipline/set boundaries
- Are consistent/dependable
- Set good examples/model what he or she teaches

- Available and profoundly involved in my life
- Aware of my emotional needs
- Able to listen without prejudging

Some of us have wonderful parents, and some of us don't. The good qualities we've been talking about are all too often absent in today's families. Rather than dislike (or even hate) our parents, we must recognize ourselves as the adopted children of our perfect heavenly Parent—Father God.

- Distribute "What's Your Story?" handout.
- Have students complete the page.
- Then discuss their answers with the understanding that all their comments need to be kept confidential within the group.

TEAM EFFORT

15 Minutes

- Distribute "Knowing Father God" handout.
- Have students form smaller groups, and assign three to four verses from the handout to each small group.
- Have them look up their assigned verses and find the matching statements describing the nature of Father God.
- After they have finished, have each small group read their verses and the appropriate statements to the whole group.

Answers to handout: (1) g, (2) d, (3) a, (4) j, (5) c, (6) e, (7) b, (8) f, (9) i, (10) h.

IN THE WORD

15 Minutes

There are responsibilities, blessings and privileges involved in our new relationship with Father God. Some of these things involve action on our part. Some of them simply involve our allowing God to work within us.

- Distribute "Father God's Loving Instructions" handout.
- After students have completed handout, discuss the instructions and guidelines found in these verses that would help them make more room for Father God in their lives.
- Discuss their responses and reactions to the questions, stressing that God's rules are for our good, and we should allow Him to help us change into godly people.
- Read Romans 12:1,2, and discuss the following:

What is your responsibility in becoming the new person? What is Father God's part in transforming us into His likeness?

Sometimes, when we are young, we feel like second-class citizens in God's family. Some older people don't seem to like us. They may even think we are always causing trouble. God has a special message even for the youngest members of His adopted family:

Don't let anyone think less of you because you are young. Be an example to all believers in what you teach, in the way you live, in your love, your faith and your purity (1 Timothy 4:12).

How does this encourage you? How does it challenge you?

FATHER GOD
REFLECTION TIME

5 Minutes

The following is a quiet, thoughtful activity that encourages students to reflect upon God's personal parenting in their lives. If possible, dim the lights in the room and ask each person to close his or her eyes. Guide the time with the following:

Our first step in reparenting ourselves is to imagine ourselves as little children in our parents' home. Do you remember what your home felt like when you were a little child? Take a moment or two and try to remember.

Now imagine yourself at your present age, walking through the front door of your house—the house you were in when you were still a little child. But instead of stepping into the presence of your parents and the way they were back then, you will step into the presence of Father God. What does He do? What does He say to you?

- After a few minutes, invite students to share their reparenting experience.

Father God has welcomed us into His family. He wants to instruct us in His ways; He wants to transform us into the image of His Son; and He wants to love us like we've never been loved before. He also wants us to know that He believes in us, so He has especially entrusted us with the responsibility of carrying His message of love to the world. That's how much confidence He has in His adopted children!

- Distribute Father God handout.

CLOSING PRAYER

Invite students to form small groups of three or four. Ask small groups to pray for one another that the areas in which they need reparenting will be brought to their attention. Then invite Father God to reparent each person in his or her area of need.

What Is Your Story?

1. What are your parents' greatest strengths?

2. What are your parents' greatest weaknesses?

3. In what area or areas of your life do you want to invite Father God to reparent you?

4. When I think of going to Father God and talking to Him about my problems, I imagine Him . . .

I think He would say . . .

"Abba, Father," [Jesus] said. Mark 14:36 (NIV)

Session 12

Knowing Father God

What kind of a parent is Father God? Through Scripture, let's get better acquainted with the parenting qualities of God, our Father. Look up the verses and match them to the statements that describe Him.

Our Father God . . .

a. Philippians 4:6,7

b. Matthew 6:8,9

c. Colossians 2:6

d. 1 Peter 5:7

e. Romans. 12:1,2

f. Ephesians 3:19,20

g. 2 Corinthians 1:3

h. 2 Corinthians 5:20,21

i. Acts 1:8

j. Galatians 3:27,28

___ 1. Is emotionally involved with us, expressing compassion, tender mercy and encouragement

___ 2. Shares our joys, hurts and cares

___ 3. Wants us to pray to Him as our Father

___ 4. Desires us to model our lives after His Son

___ 5. Joins us with Jesus

___ 6. Wants us to know and do His will

___ 7. Wants to meet our needs

___ 8. Has made available to us the same power that raised Jesus from the dead to live a life that brings honor to the Father.

___ 9. Wants us to love, serve and proclaim His kingdom in the world.

___10. Want us to be His ambassadors to share Father God with others

> *You should behave instead like God's very own children, adopted into his family—calling him "Father, dear Father." For His Holy Spirit speaks to us deep in our hearts and tells us that we are God's children. And since we are His children, we will share His treasures—for everything God gives to His Son, Christ, is ours too.*
> **Romans 8:15,16**

Session 12

Father God's Loving Instructions

Page 1

In the following Scripture quotations, underline the verbs (i.e., "do," "don't," "be," "get," etc.) that tell you to do something. Then put a circle around the word "let" where ever you find it.

Let heaven fill your thoughts. Do not think only about things down here on earth. For you died when Christ died, and your real life is hidden with Christ in God. And when Christ, who is your real life, is revealed to the whole world, you will share in all his glory.

So put to death the sinful, earthly things lurking within you. Have nothing to do with sexual sin, impurity, lust, and shameful desires. Don't be greedy for the good things of this life, for that is idolatry. But now is the time to get rid of anger, rage, malicious behavior, slander, and dirty language.

Don't lie to each other, for you have stripped off your old evil nature and all its wicked deeds. In its place you have clothed yourselves with a brand-new nature that is continually being renewed as you learn more and more about Christ, who created this new nature within you.

Since God chose you to be the holy people whom he loves, you must clothe yourselves with tenderhearted mercy, kindness, humility, gentleness, and patience. You must make allowance for each other's faults and forgive the person who offends you. Remember, the Lord forgave you, so you must forgive others. And the most important piece of clothing you must wear is love. Love is what binds us all together in perfect harmony.

And let the peace that comes from Christ rule in your hearts. For as members of one body you are all called to live in peace. And always be thankful. Let the words of Christ, in all their richness, live in your hearts and make you wise. Use his words to teach and counsel each other. Sing psalms and hymns and spiritual songs to God with thankful hearts. And whatever you do or say, let it be as a representative of the Lord Jesus, all the while giving thanks through him to God the Father. Colossians 3:2-5,8-10,12-17

Session 12

Father God's Loving Instructions

Page 2

1. Does being part of Father God's family just mean keeping a bunch of new rules?

2. Do we have to do everything perfectly so He'll keep loving us?

3. Does God change us instantly or in a process?

4. Are there rules of conduct in other relationships in our lives? Explain.

5. What is the purpose for God's instructions—are they for His benefit or for ours?

6. Does God get mad at us when we don't do what He says we should do?

> *Because you are sons, God sent the Spirit of his Son into our hearts, the Spirit who calls out, "Abba, Father."* Galatians 4:6 (*NIV*)

Session 12

 FATHER GOD

Jesus came and told his disciples, "I have been given complete authority in heaven and on earth. Therefore, go and make disciples of all the nations, baptizing them in the name of the Father and the Son and the Holy Spirit. Teach these new disciples to obey all the commands I have given you. And be sure of this; I am with you always, even to the end of the age."
Matthew 28:18-20

Once you have become an adopted member of Father God's family, He has given you the privilege of bringing others to know Him too. This may sound difficult, or it may sound like an exciting opportunity. Tell Father God how you feel about the Great Commission He has given to all of His children.

Dear Father God,

Love,
Your Adopted Child

CONFIDENTIALITY AGREEMENT

Our program today will include some worksheets and discussions that may involve personal information. Because we respect one another's privacy, and need to feel safe in our group, let's make a commitment to confidentiality so we can fully trust one another with whatever may be said.

I, _____ , promise to keep confidential anything that is said here today by any participant. I will not share with anyone outside of this present group anything that is discussed.

Signed,

_____

Dated _____

Appendix B

NARTH Fact Sheet

Many laymen now believe that homosexuality is a part of *who a person really is*—from the moment of conception.

The genetic and unchangeable theory has been actively promoted by gay activists and the popular media. Is homosexuality really an inborn and normal variant of human nature?

No. There is no evidence that shows that homosexuality is genetic. **And none of the research claims there is.** Only the press and certain researchers do, when speaking in sound bites to the public.

HOW THE PUBLIC WAS MISLED

In July of 1993, the prestigious research journal *Science* published a study by Dean Hamer which claims that there might be a gene for homosexuality. Research seemed to be on the verge of proving that homosexuality is innate, genetic and therefore unchangeable—a normal variant of human nature.

Soon afterward, National Public Radio trumpeted those findings. *Newsweek* ran the cover story, "Gay Gene?" *The Wall Street Journal* announced, "Research Points Toward a Gay Gene . . . Normal Variation."

Of course, certain necessary qualifiers were added within those news stories. But only an expert knew what those qualifiers meant. The vast majority of readers were urged to believe that homosexuals had been proved to be "born that way."

In order to grasp what is really going on, one needs to understand some little-known facts about behavioral genetics.

GENE LINKAGE STUDIES

Dean Hamer and his colleagues had performed a common type of behavioral genetics investigation called the "linkage study." Researchers identify a behavioral trait that runs in a family, and then:

a) look for a chromosomal variant in the genetic material of that family, and

b) determine whether that variant is more frequent in family members who share the particular trait.

To the layman, the "correlation" of a genetic structure with a behavioral trait means that trait "is genetic"—in other words, *inherited.*

In fact, it means absolutely nothing of the sort, and it should be emphasized that there is virtually no human trait without innumberable such correlations.

SCIENTISTS KNOW THE TRUTH ABOUT "GAY GENE" RESEARCH

But before we consider the specifics, here is what serious scientists think about recent genetics-of-behavior research. From *Science*, 1994:

> Time and time again, scientists have claimed that particular genes or chromosomal regions are associated with behavioral traits, only to withdraw their findings when they were not replicated. "Unfortunately," says Yale's [Dr. Joel] Gelernter, "It's hard to come up with many findings linking specific genes to complex human behaviors that have been replicated. All were announced with great fanfare; all were greeted unskeptically in the popular press; all are now in disrepute."[1]

HOMOSEXUAL TWIN STUDIES

Two American activists recently published studies showing that if one of a pair of identical twins is homosexual, the other member of the pair will be, too, in just under 50% of the cases. On this basis, they claim that "homosexuality is genetic".

But two other genetic researchers—one heads one of the largest genetics departments in the country, the other is at Harvard—comment:

> While the authors interpreted their findings as evidence for a genetic basis for homosexuality, we think that the data in fact provide strong evidence for the influence of the environment.[2]

The author of the lead article on genes and behavior in a special issue of *Science* speaks of the renewed scientific recognition of the importance of environment. He notes the growing understanding that:

> . . . the interaction of genes and environment is much more complicated than the simple "violence genes" and "intelligence genes" touted in the popular press. The same data that show the effects of genes, also point to the enormous influence of non-genetic factors.[3]

MORE MODEST CLAIMS TO THE SCIENTIFIC COMMUNITY

Researchers' public statements to the press are often grand and far-reaching. But when answering the scientific community, they speak much more cautiously.

"Gay gene" researcher Dean Hamer was asked by *Scientific American* if homosexuality was rooted solely in biology. He replied:

> "Absolutely not. From twin studies, we already know that half or more of the variability in sexual orientation is not inherited. Our studies try to pinpoint the genetic factors . . . not negate the psychosocial factors."[4]

But in qualifying their findings, researchers often use language that will surely evade general understanding—making statements that will continue to be avoided by the popular press, such as:

> . . . the question of the appropriate significance level to apply to a non-Mendelian trait such as sexual orientation is problematic.[5]

Sounds too complex to bother translating? This is actually a very important statement. In layman's terms, this means:

> It is *not possible* to know what the findings mean—*if anything*—since sexual orientation cannot possibly be inherited in the direct way eye-color is.

Thus, to their fellow scientists, the researchers have been honestly acknowledging the limitations of their research. However, **the media doesn't understand that message.** Columnist Ann Landers, for example, tells her readers that "homosexuals are born, not made." The media offers partial truths because the scientific reality is simply too unexciting to make the evening news; too complex for mass consumption; and furthermore, not fully and accurately understood by reporters.

ACCURATE REPORTING WILL NEVER COME IN "SOUND BITES"

There are no "lite," sound-bite versions of behavioral genetics that are not fundamentally in error in one way or another.

Nonetheless, if one grasps at least some of the basics, in simple form, it will be possible to see exactly why the current research methods improve—so long as it remains driven by political, rather than scientific objectives.

UNDERSTANDING THE THEORY

There are only two major principles that need to be carefully understood in order to see through the distortions of the recent research. They are as follows:

1. *Heritable* does not meant *inheritable.*
2. Genetics research which is truly meaningful will identify, and then focus on, only traits that are *directly inherited.*

Almost every human characteristic is in significant measure *heritable*. But few human behavioral traits are directly *inherited,* in the manner of height, for example, or eye color. *Inherited* means "directly determined by genes," with little or no way of preventing or modifying the trait through a change in the environment.

HOW TO "PROVE" THAT BASKETBALL PLAYERS ARE BORN THAT WAY

Suppose you are motivated to demonstrate—for political reasons—that there is a basketball gene that makes people grow up to be basketball players. You would use the same methods that have been used with homosexuality: (1) twin studies; (2) brain dissections; (3) gene "linkage" studies.

The basic idea in twin studies is to show that the more genetically similar two people are, the more likely it is that they will share the trait you are studying.

So you identify groups of twins in which at least one person is a a basketball player. You will probably find that if one identical twin is a basketball player, his twin brother is statistically more likely to be one, too. You would need to create groups of different kinds of pairs to make further comparisons—one set of identical twin pairs, one set of non-identical twin pairs, one set of sibling pairs, etc.

Using the "concordance rate" (the percentage of pairs in which both twins are basketball players, or both are not), you would calculate a "heritability" rate. The concordance rate would be quite high—just as in the concordance rate for homosexuality.

Then, you announce to the reporter from *Sports Illustrated:* "Our research demonstrates that basketball playing is strongly heritable." (And you would be right. It would be "heritable"—but not directly inherited. Few readers would be aware of the distinction, however.)

Soon after, the article appears. It says: "New research shows that basketball playing is probably inherited. Basketball players are apparently 'born that way'! A number of outside researchers examined the work and found it substantially accurate and well-performed."

But no one (other than the serious scientist) notices the media's inaccurate reporting.

WHAT ALL NEUROLOGISTS KNOW: THE BRAIN CHANGES WITH USE

Then you move on to conduct some brain research. As in the well-known LeVay brain study which measured parts of the hypothalamus, your colleagues perform a series of autopsies on the brains of some dead people who, they have reason to believe, were basketball players.

Next, they do the same with a group of dead nonbasketball players. Your colleagues report that, on average, "Certain parts of the brain long thought to be involved with basketball playing are much larger in the group of basketball players."

A few national newspapers pick up on the story and editorialize, *"Clearly, basketball playing is not a choice.* Not only does basketball playing run in families, but even the player's [sic] *brains* are different."

You, of course, as a scientist, are well aware that the brain changes with use. . . *indeed quite dramatically.* Those parts responsible for an activity get larger over time, and there are specific parts of the brain that are more utilized in basketball playing.

Now, as a scientist, you will not **lie** about this fact, *if asked* (since you will not be), but neither will you go out of your way to offer the truth. The truth, after all, would put an end to the worldwide media blitz accompanying the announcement of your findings.

GENE LINKAGE STUDIES: "ASSOCIATED WITH" DOES NOT MEAN "CAUSED BY"

Now, for the last phase, you find a small number of families of basketball players and compare them to some families of non-players. You have a hunch that of the innumerable genes likely to be associated with basketball playing (those for height, athleticism, and quick reflexes, for example), some will be located on the x-chromosome.

You won't say these genes *cause* basketball playing because such a claim would be scientifically insupportable, but the public thinks "caused by" and "associated with" are synonymous.

After a few false starts, sure enough, you find what you are looking for: among the basketball-playing families, one particular cluster of genes is found more commonly.

WITH A LITTLE HELP FROM THE MEDIA

Now, it happens that you have some sympathizers at National People's Radio. Commentators pontificate about the enormous public-policy implications of this superb piece of science. Two weeks later, there it is again, on the cover of the major national newsweekly: "Basketball Gene?"

Now what is wrong with this scenario? It is simple: they were long ago quietly informed of your research. They want people to come around to certain beliefs, too. So, as soon as your work hits the press, they are on the air: ***"Researchers are hot on the trail of the Basketball Gene . . . In an article to be published tomorrow in Sports Science*** basketball playing is associated with certain genes; of course it is heritable." But it is those intermediate physiological traits—muscle strength, speed, agility, reflex speed, height, etc.—which are themselves directly inherited. Those are the traits that make it likely one will be able to, and will want to, play basketball.

In the case of homosexuality, the inherited traits that are more common among male homosexuals might include a greater-than-average tendency to anxiety, shyness, sensitivity, intelligence, and aesthetic abilities. But this is speculation. To date, researchers have not yet sought to identify these factors with scientific rigor.

IN SUMMARY

The majority of respected scientists now believe that homosexuality is attributable to a combination of **psychological, social, and biological factors.**

From the American Psychological Association

"[M]any scientists share the view that sexual orientation is shaped for most people at an early age through complex interactions of biological, psychological and social factors."[6]

From "Gay Brain Researcher" Simon LeVay

"At this point, the most widely held opinion [on causation of homosexuality] is that *multiple factors* play a role."[7]

From Sociologist Steven Goldberg

"**I know of no one** in the field who argues that homosexuality can be explained without reference to environmental factors."[8]

As we have seen, there is no evidence that homosexuality is genetic— and none of the research claims there is.

Only the press and certain researchers do, when speaking in sound bites to the public.

Endnotes

1. Mann, C. Genes and behavior. *Science* 264:1687 (1994).

2. Billings, P. and Beckwith, J. *Technology Review*, July, 1993. p. 60.

3. Mann, C. op.cit. pp.1686-1689.

4. "Gay Genes, Revisited: Doubts arise over research on the biology of homosexuality," *Scientific American*, November 1995, p. 26.

5. Hamer, D.H., et al. *Response to Risch*, N., et al. loc. cit.

6. The American Psychological Association's pamphlet, "Answers to Your Questions About Sexual Orientation and Homosexuality":

7. LeVay, Simon, (1996). *Queer Science*, MIT Press.

8. Goldberg, Steven (1994). *When Wish Replaces Thought: Why So Much of What You Believe is False*. Buffalo, New York: Prometheus Books.

This article was adapted by permission from two sources: a paper entitled, "The Gay Gene?" by Jeffrey Satinover, M.D., in The Journal of Human Sexuality, 1996, available by calling (972) 713-7130; and past issues of the National Association of Research and Therapy of Homosexuality (NARTH) Bulletin. For an in-depth discussion of homosexuality and genetics, consult Dr. Satinover's 1996 book, Homosexuality and the Politics of Truth, published by Hamewith/Baker Books.

Appendix C
For Further Reading

Allender and Longman. *Bold Love*. Colorado Springs: NavPress, 1992.
    Chapters include: Know the Difference Between Loving an Evil Person, a Fool and a Normal Sinner; What It Means to "Honor" a Wicked Parent; Why Anger Usually Outlives Forgiveness; How to Love an Abusive Person Without Opening Yourself Up to Damage.

Arterburn, Steve, and Jim Burns. *Drugproof Your Kids*. Ventura, CA: Regal Books, 1995.

Cloud, Henry, and John Townsend. *The Mom-Factor*. Grand Rapids: Zondervan, 1996.

Dallas, Joe. A Strong Delusion: *Confronting the "Gay Christian" Movement*. Eugene, OR: Harvest House, 1996.

Davies, Lori, and R. Rentzeld. *Coming Out of Homosexuality*. Downers Grove, IL: InterVarsity Press, 1996.

Dobson, James. *Love Must Be Tough*. Dallas: Word Publishing, 1983.

Harvey, John F. O. S. F.S. *The Truth About Homosexuality: The Cry of the Faithful*. San Francisco: Ignatius, 1996.

LaHaye, Tim, and Phillips, Bob. *Anger Is a Choice*. Grand Rapids: Zondervan, 1982.

Lewis, C.S. *Mere Christianity*. New York: Macmillan, 1986.

Mawyer, Martin. *Silent Shame*. Westchester, IL: Crossway Books, 1987."
    "The Alarming Rise of Child Sexual Abuse and How to Protect Your Children From It"

Nicolosi, Joseph. *Reparative Therapy of Male Homosexuality*. Norvale, NJ: Jason Aronson, 1991.

Olson, Joe. *When Passions Are Confused: Understanding Homosexuality*. Grand Rapids: Radio Bible Class Ministries.
    This booklet may be suitable for some young people, but should first be reviewed by leadership.

Rekers, George A. *Handbook of Child and Adolescent Sexual Problems*. New York: Lexington Books, 1995.

Rentzel, Lori. *Emotional Dependency* (booklet). Downers Grove: InterVarsity Press, 1990.

Satinover, Jeffrey, M.D. *Homosexuality and the Politics of Truth.* Grand Rapids: Baker Books, 1996.

Schmidt, Thomas E. *Straight & Narrow? Compassion & Clarity in the Homosexual Debate.* Downers Grove: InterVarsity Press, 1995.

Schmierer, Don. *An Ounce of Prevention.* Nashville: Word Publishing, 1998.

Snider, Ron. *Genuine Christianity.* Grand Rapids: Zondervan, 1996.

Socarides, Charles W., M.D. *Homosexuality: A Freedom Too Far.* Phoenix: Adam Margrave Books, 1995.

Stewart, V. Mary. *Sexual Freedom* (booklet). Downers Grove: InterVarsity Press, 1974.

Stott, John. *Basic Christianity.* Downers Grove: InterVarsity Press, 1971.

Wilson, Bill. *Whose Child Is This?* Lake Mary, FL: Creation House, 1992.

Wooding, Dan. *He Intends Victory.* Irvine, CA: Promise Publishing, 1994.

Worthen and Davies. *Someone I Love Is Gay.* Downers Grove: InterVarsity Press, 1996.

Yancey, Philip. *Disappointment with God.* Grand Rapids: Zondervan, 1988.